CONCILIUM

Religion in the Eighties

CONCILIUM

Concilium 172 (2/1984): Moral Theology

CONCILIUM

THE ETHICS OF LIBERATION—
THE LIBERATION OF ETHICS

Edited by
Dietmar Mieth
Jacques Pohier

English Language Editor
Marcus Lefébure

T. & T. CLARK LTD
Edinburgh

April 1984
T. & T. Clark Ltd, 36 George Street, Edinburgh EH2 2LQ
ISBN: 0 567 30052 8

ISSN: 0010-5236

Typeset by C. R. Barber & Partners (Highlands) Ltd, Fort William
Printed by Blackwood, Pillans & Wilson Ltd, Edinburgh

Concilium: Published February, April, June, August, October, December.
Subscriptions 1984: UK £19.00; USA $40.00; Canada $50.00; Rest of the World £19.00.
Postage and packing included.

CONTENTS

Part III
Towards a Dialogue between the Ethic of Autonomy and the Ethic of Liberation

Part IV
Documentation

Editorial:
Ethics and the Challenge of Liberation

ANYONE EXAMINING the claims of liberation in modern ethics will immediately come up against the concept of autonomy. Since the Enlightenment and the 'Secularisation' [1802–3 in Germany], 'autonomy' has been the fundamental perspective of philosophical anthropology and ethics. And since the Second Vatican Council it has also been seen as a fundamental Christian option, although the particular relevance of autonomy in the Christian context is a matter of dispute. In attempting to integrate 'autonomy' into theology, we find ourselves in close proximity to philosophers involved with the question of God. Is freedom 'one way of conceiving God' (H. Krings)?

The concept of autonomy is highly vulnerable to misunderstanding. For some it smacks of atheism, for others it is connected with the rejection of ecclesiastical authority; some see it as a hedonistic ideology for a consumer society, while to many it is merely a slogan of European/North American individualism. Furthermore, the ethics of autonomy has not put a stop to exploitation and misery on the fringes of society. Is autonomy perhaps only an ideology for power-centres?

So we ask: What conclusions can be drawn, in existential and political terms, from our experience of autonomy? How can we distinguish between an authentic ethics of autonomy and its abuses? Is not an ethics built on autonomy too abstract? Does it not create a tension between the concept of freedom and the experience of it? Is not political liberation necessary before we can experience and realise ethical autonomy?

If we survey the development of Christian social ethics in the last twenty years—including the documents of the *magisterium*—we come across 'liberation' more and more as a fundamental anthropological and ethical option. The experience of liberation is seen as a Christian inheritance in the context of the oppressed, in the social praxis of Christian basic communities, in the understanding of evangelisation, in the idea of a new ecclesiology, and finally in the idea of social justice. Opting for liberation, however, is also liable to be gravely misunderstood. Some regard it as a consequence of political emancipation, springing from the same root as 'autonomy'. They fear a confusion of Gospel and politics. Others are disquieted by a revolution in the Church's tradition. Again, others are afraid that a praxis of liberation which shows partiality will cause a breach in love's universality. A few, finally, regard it as the eschatological sugar on the pill of militant action.

Here too there are questions: What have been the results of liberation in existential and political terms? How can we distinguish between an authentic ethics of liberation and its abuses? Does not an ethics based on total liberation promise more than it can deliver?

Such questions clearly show the absolute necessity of a dialogue between autonomous ethics (centred on the First World) and an ethics of liberation (centred on the liberation theology of the Third World): without this, there can be no agreement between Christians on ethics, and in particular on what constitutes the Christian dimension in ethics. The basis for such a dialogue are the scriptures of the Old and New Testaments, but also the living tradition of freedom movements in the Church. Here too the reflections of philosophical ethics are important, as is the experience which praxis yields. Finally there is the criterion of the consequences which flow from these concepts and influence people's way of life and social institutions. i.e., the whole area of ethical norms.

It would be impossible, within the compass of one issue of *Concilium* to present a full treatment of all the various perspectives. What follows is an attempt to get the dialogue started, at least in broad outline. The first part is concerned with the concept of autonomy and the way it has been dealt with in Christian ethics. P. Rossi endeavours to dismantle the misunderstandings arising from a liberalist position vis-a-vis Kant's concept of autonomy. K. Hilpert describes the various theological reactions to autonomy and their influence. B. Quelquejeu shows how the problem of the 'question of God' was solved in the French philosophy of reflection. V. Eid discusses the methodological significance of 'autonomy' in dealing with concrete ethical questions.

Part two describes the development (F. Moreno Rejón) and substance (E. Dussel) of a Christian liberation ethics. A. Moser shows how the context of liberation ethics transforms the way God is seen, and its effects on the Church's socio-ethical and pastoral documents are presented by T. Mifsud.

Part three concerns the dialogue between autonomy and liberation. The basis for this dialogue is the testimony of scripture (L. Schottroff). In the Bible, freedom and unfreedom are concrete matters. The experience of freedom is always the experience of the liberated man. D. Stein indicates how difficult it is to give an exact description of autonomy as the goal of psychoanalytic liberation, where the individual is faced with a multiplicity of social ties. (Here, unfortunately, in spite of strenuous efforts, we have been unable to come up with a contribution based on the experience of political liberation praxis. This shows once again how hard it is to find competent Third World writers who are in touch with the practical, political and pastoral realities.)

M. Vidal tries to develop the dialogue between autonomy and liberation into an ethics of solidarity in the emancipation process. D. Mieth endeavours to show how, in a Christian context, an autonomous ethics can justify its claim to be an analytic reflection on moral judgment, while at the same time being involved in a learning process through contact with the Christian ethos of liberation.

Inevitably, this issue of *Concilium* contains a lot of information and makes considerable demands of the reader. Our idea was that it could be used as basic source material for further work, and as a stimulus to dialogue. Therefore we have appended some documentation in the form of select bibliographies, with commentary, on autonomous ethics (A. Bondolfi) and liberation ethics (M. C. Morkovsky). We are particularly glad to find that the authors represented here, without being aware of each other's contributions, have unwittingly worked in the same direction, often raising the same problems. May all this help us to come to a deeper grasp of the nature of Christian ethics.

DIETMAR MIETH
JACQUES POHIER

Translated by Graham Harrison

PART I

The Christian Ethic:
An Ethic of Autonomy?

Philip Rossi

The Foundation of the Philosophical Concept of Autonomy by Kant and its Historical Consequences

I

IMMANUEL KANT'S *Groundwork of the Metaphysic of Morals*[1] published in 1785, is generally acknowledged as one of the classic texts of Western moral philosophy. Like most classic texts, it has a richness of thought that lends itself to a variety of interpretations. One line of interpretation, however, has played a particularly important role even to the present day in giving shape to discussions of moral theory and to the practice of the moral life both in Europe and in the English speaking world. That interpretation takes its focus on the notion of autonomy which, as its very etymology (*auto-* self; *nomos-* law) suggests, has fundamental reference to the power of the human rational will to make law for itself.

There can be little doubt that Kant himself understood autonomy to be central for his account of human moral life: in the *Groundwork* he labels autonomy of the will as the supreme principle of morality.[2] Yet the authority of Kant by no means accounts for the prominent role autonomy—and related notions that focus on the power of the human self to formulate and follow principles of action—have played in subsequent philosophical discussions and in determining the shape of moral practice. Within this larger cultural context, Kant's articulation of the notion of autonomy can be viewed as the philosophical crystallisation of a concern that the Enlightenment made central to its programme and that Kant himself called both an 'inclination' and a 'vocation': human freedom in thought and action.[3]

My procedure in this essay will be to sketch out two perspectives on autonomy which have been opened by recent scholarship. The one I shall first sketch takes focus on the role that the notion of autonomy has played in giving shape to moral theory since the time of Kant. This perspective—which I find most powerfully and persuasively framed in Alasdair MacIntyre's *After Virtue*[4]—makes it plain that selves created in the image of autonomy by the political culture of liberalism cannot sustain a common moral world in which to dwell. Autonomy, viewed from this perspective, has brought us to a moral dead end, where a rhetoric of putatively rational moral discourse masks over the engagement of the particular and arbitrary interests of our individual wills in a never-ending contest for

3

mastery. Only a bold few indeed—such as Kafka and Nietzsche—have faced squarely the consequences of our coming to this dead end.

The self that this perspective describes is, undoubtedly, a self shaped by a culturally pervasive notion of autonomy. As I hope my sketch of the second perspective will suggest, however, a notion of autonomy that shapes a self unable to sustain a common moral world in which to dwell is not Kant's notion of autonomy. His understanding of autonomy, as a number of recent studies have started to note,[5] places it in a context that requires human moral agents to sustain a common moral world both for the intelligibility and for the proper exercise of the law making power of their rational wills.

In sketching out these two perspectives I have a two-fold aim: the first is to show that MacIntyre and others, in their criticism of an autonomy conceived as isolated from human social and historical reality, have located a basic misapprehension that has taken deep and destructive root in much contemporary moral self-understanding. This misapprehension consists in taking human freedom, as it is exercised in the decisions and choices of autonomous moral agents, to stand in opposition to the constraints on decision and choices that arise from the human condition of interdependence, mutuality, and temporality.

My second aim is to propose one place from which the work of correcting this misapprehension can start. In view of the face that Kant is usually seen as the progenitor of this misapprehension, the starting point I propose will seem paradoxical, since it is Kant's own account of autonomy. I propose Kant's account as this starting point in consequence of the findings of recent scholarship; some of Kant's commentators have started to take note of features of his work, frequently overlooked in the past, that call into question those interpretations of autonomy that make its focus the will of the individual which, in order to be rational in making moral decisions, must prescind from the conditions of time and of human mutuality. This same scholarship suggests, moreover, that an interpretation of autonomy that is faithfully drawn to the contours of Kant's own account will show a common moral world to be both starting point and final term of that exercise of human finite reason which Kant calls 'autonomy'.

This reinterpretation of Kant's account of autonomy, by recovering the fundamental reference that account has to a world that exhibits human mutuality and interdependence, offers, in my judgment, one appropriate place on which to focus the dialogue between the ethics of autonomy and the ethics of liberation that this volume seeks to initiate. It offers an appropriate focus inasmuch as it opens a possibility for establishing a mutually foundational relationship between the fundamental concerns—human freedom and human solidarity—that have given shape, respectively, to the ethics of autonomy and the ethics of liberation.

II

There is a measure of truth in the insight that the interpretations we give to classic works of literature, philosophy, or religion tell us at least as much about ourselves, the interpreters, as they do about the texts we interpret. So it has been in the case of Kant. Through his focus on autonomy we have no difficulty seeing the lineaments of the political culture that has held sway in the North Atlantic basin for much of the last two centuries: the culture that has been embodied in the social, political, and economic institutions of liberal democracy.

We find Kant's account of autonomy to be an appropriate focus because through it we seem to catch sight of a clear image of the self that is suited to live and to flourish under such institutions. Iris Murdoch has provided a most apt portrait of the image we see:

How recognizable, how familiar to us, is the man so beautifully portrayed in the *Groundwork*, who confronted even with Christ turns away to consider the judgment of his own conscience and to hear the voice of his reason. . . . [T]his man is with us still, free, independent, lonely, powerful, rational, responsible, brave, the hero of so many novels and books of moral philosophy. . . . He is the ideal citizen of the liberal State, a warning held up to tyrants.[6]

In viewing this image, Murdoch notes, moreover, one detail most of us who are heirs to this culture are apt to overlook: 'Kant's man had already received a glorious incarnation nearly a century earlier in the work of Milton: His proper name is Lucifer.'[7]

We are most apt to name freedom as the characteristic that makes the self formed in this image suited to live and flourish in the culture of liberal democracy; the freedom we would so designate, moreover, is taken to consist in the power of rational individuals to make autonomous choices. The analyses of critics such as MacIntyre, Murdoch, and Stanley Hauerwas[8] have helped bring to light why this characteristic can be deemed so appropriate for the ideal citizen of the liberal State: through the power of autonomous choice, a human moral agent gives expression to the self-sufficiency that constitutes the inner and irreducible core of what MacIntyre has aptly called a modern 'invention': the individual.[9] Although many factors played a role in the invention of the individual, there is only one we need consider in this essay. The modern notion of the individual becomes possible once we believe that we can picture the self as free from the particularities of history and of human community. Once this picture has us in its grip, the power of the human rational will to make law for itself is transmuted into the possibility of human will being a law unto itself: autonomy becomes autarchy. There is a notable irony here: autonomy, which Kant intended to portray as the way in which the self expressed the inherent rationality of the moral order and by which the self held itself accountable to that order turns out to be, instead, the paradigmatic exercise of a wilfulness immune to rational accountability.

This irony has not been confined, moreover, to the conceptual order. It has also been playing itself out in various realms of our culture's public life; it appears in its most vexing form as the problem of providing an adequate and coherent understanding of the very possibility of public life for a polity constituted by and as an aggregation of individuals who, by the very terms of the definition of the political order, must be conceived as intent upon the pursuit and satisfaction of their own interests. Parker Palmer has put the problem well:

The mainstream of our political thought has assumed that the individual, by nature, is primarily motivated by self-interest. If that is true, then a public is possible, only as ways are found to correlate and control the vast diversity of self-interests. The task of government is to provide a framework of rules and penalties within which a community can be constructed out of the convergence of self-interests, with those interests that do not fit being deflected or simply denied. In this stream of political theory, the public has been reduced to an arena in which individuals compete for the most they can get with the government as the referee.[10]

Autonomy seems thus to have engendered a world in which we must face one another as strangers and, as Palmer has noted, we cannot enter such a world 'without being (literally and figuratively) well-armed'.[11] We face one another as strangers in consequence of the way we have put autonomy into practice: we have taken it to place the sole source of moral authority in the individual and thus to require, for the moral integrity of our choices, that they be made in independence from the constraints which the particularities of history and of human community place upon us.

The world of strangers which our practice of autonomy has constituted can justly be interpreted as a most manifest sign of a fundamental misreading of a basic reality that constitutes us in our identity as members of the same human species: finite rational freedom. The very freedom we should acknowledge as fundamental ground of our identity with one another seems instead to have set us apart from and in opposition to one another.

III

The sketch presented in the preceding section undoubtedly suggests that the legacy bestowed on us, under the title of autonomy, has proved corrosive of our sense of having a share in a common humanity. In this final section, I hope to show that such corrosive power is not inherent in Kant's own account of autonomy. It is not the legacy itself, but how we have used it—in opposition to Kant's own intent—that has led us to turn autonomy into the moral self-sufficiency that strangers need to deal with one another. I hope to show that, on Kant's own account, the exercise of autonomy, rather than making us strangers to one another, instead gives expression to a commitment to dwell in a shared moral world. One of the more notable phrases Kant employs to characterise human moral existence—the membership of all rational agents in a 'kingdom of ends'[12]—more than hints at such a commitment; yet seldom has this hint been picked up or developed by interpretations commonly given to Kant's moral philosophy; even more rarely has it influenced the practices by which autonomy has become enshrined as a highly individualistic notion.

There are many reasons why this commitment to dwell in a shared moral world has failed often to play a prominent role in interpretations of Kant's ethics or, for that matter, in the determination of conduct that could be considered to exemplify 'autonomy'. One reason, surely, is that Kant, particularly in his most widely read work in moral philosophy, the *Groundwork*, does not offer a thematically explicit or systematically developed treatment of such a commitment. Moreover, when he does make the community of moral agents explicitly the focus of his discussion—for instance, in Book Three of *Religion Within the Limits of Reason Alone*[13]—he does not clearly spell out all its systematic connections with each moral agent's exercise of autonomy.

Kant, nonetheless, need not be burdened with all the responsibility for neglect of this dimension of his account of autonomy. It has come about also in consequence of the tendency, particularly within the English-speaking philosophical world, to make Kant's concern as expressed in the *Critique of Pure Reason*, namely, to mark off the boundaries for reason in its speculative use, the principal interpretive focus from which to view his accounts of morality and of religion. A number of recent explorations of Kant's work, however, have opened possibilities for taking a different perspective in interpreting both Kant's project of constructing a critical philosophy and the role his accounts of morality and of religion play in that critical project. The central focus for this interpretation is the answer Kant works out, in the course of elaborating his critical philosophy, to the last of the three famous questions he posed to set the goal for his inquiry into the scope and function of human reason: 'What can I know? What ought I to do? What may I hope?'[14] The question of hope is central to Kant's critical project inasmuch as he himself conceived it as a question about the unity of the two uses—for theory and for practice—to which the dynamics of human reason order its exercise. More particularly, the question of hope is a question about the fundamental unity of human existence as it finds itself located at the juncture of the world of nature, whose order takes form in accord with principles elaborated in scientific inquiry, and the world of freedom, whose order takes form in accord with principles exhibited in and by the moral governance of human action.

Kant frames his answer to the question of hope in terms of a concept of 'highest good'. Although there is a number of vexing problems with the terms and the arguments Kant uses in delimiting this concept, there can be little doubt that he understood it to function as a necessary completion of his account of human autonomy; thus, in the *Critique of Practical Reason* he refers to the highest good as necessarily the object of pure practical reason, i.e., of autonomy.[15] The link Kant forges between the notion of the highest good and that of autonomy has particular significance for an assessment of the extent to which our current understanding of autonomy and its embodiment in various practices of our culture have remained faithful to Kant's own thinking. The significance of this link between the highest good and autonomy lies in the fact that Kant understands the highest good to take form as a fundamentally social reality; he makes a particularly explicit affirmation of this understanding in *Religion within the Limits of Reason Alone*:

> Now we have here a duty which is *sui generis*, not of men toward men, but of the human race toward itself. For the species of rational beings is, objectively, in the idea of reason, destined for a social goal, namely, the promotion of the highest as a social good.[16]

In view of the social form taken by the highest good, Kant's claim that the attainment of the highest good is necessarily the object of the exercise of human autonomy can thus be understood as also affirming a fundamentally social dimension to the power of the human rational will to make law for itself. In consequence, Kant's own characterisation of the highest good as social renders problematic those interpretations of autonomy, such as the ones prevailing in much current discussion and practice, that fail to give it an inherently social form or direction.

Three other aspects of Kant's notion of the highest good lend additional support to an interpretation of autonomy that gives it an inherently social form and direction. The first two—that our human endeavour for the attainment of the highest good takes both public and historical form—are given explicit representation and development in Kant's image of an 'ethical commonwealth'.[17] The third—that the social form and direction inherent to the exercise of reason can be traced back to the 'interest' of reason—is less explicit; it holds promise, however, of being a particularly important basis for discussion between the ethics of autonomy and the ethics of liberation. As a result, a brief consideration both of the function of the interest of reason in Kant's account of autonomy and of the possibilities this offers for such dialogue makes it an appropriate topic with which to conclude this essay.

When Kant refers to the interest of reason, he is usually speaking of our human efforts at representing some kind of all-encompassing totality.[18] Since autonomy, in Kant's view, is the form which reason takes in the governance of human/moral conduct, we should expect the exercise of autonomy to manifest this interest of reason; in particular, it manifests itself first of all in the universally binding form of moral judgment that Kant terms the 'categorical imperative'. It manifests itself also in the highest good that necessarily serves as the object of autonomy. Both these manifestations of the interest of reason serve to place human moral agents in a context that we may aptly term a 'world'. Kant's images of a kingdom of ends and an ethical commonwealth suggest, moreover, that the world into which the interest of reason places us is one constituted by our relations to each other and by all of us together as moral agents. These images offer a picture of the moral world and of the selves who dwell in that world that stands in sharp contrast to the picture we, in our day, have come to associate with autonomy. A world fashioned in accord with Kant's images is not one in which we stand first as strangers to one another and, only after negotiation, become willing to acknowledge, for some matters at least, the possibility of a common pursuit of good; it is, instead, a world in which we first acknowledge our likeness to one another as the very condition for our being moral agents.

To be sure, Kant gives an abstract characterisation—rationality—to the likeness that

B

we are to acknowledge as the basis for our dwelling in a common moral world. The abstractness of Kant's characterisation of this likeness, however, should not obscure the far more fundamental point made by these images in which the interest of reason is given concrete representation: the very intelligibility of our moral autonomy rests upon our prior acknowledgment of human commonality and communality.

In the two centuries that have passed since the publication of the *Groundwork of the Metaphysic of Morals*, the notion of autonomy has been put to many uses that have been forgetful of this most fundamental fact about this power of the human will to make law for itself: that this power not only has its ground in reason itself, but that it is the very power by which the inherently public and social character of reason—its 'interest'—is made manifest. In consequence of this forgetfulness, autonomy has come to be associated with attitudes, conduct, and practices which, in so far as they express an a-social individualism, are justly subject to criticism from the perspective of an ethics, such as that of liberation, which takes human solidarity as the starting point for moral reflection. It is my hope that the sketch I have provided of Kant's account of autonomy, by locating it in the context of a shared moral world, has indicated that such attitudes, conduct, and practices are also subject to criticism from the perspective of an ethics of autonomy: an ethics of autonomy faithful to Kant's own insights into the social character of reason and into the foundation of autonomy in our acknowledgment of a common humanity with a destiny of shared good.

Notes

1. Trans. H. J. Paton, New York 1964 (*Grundlegung zur Metaphysik der Sitten*; references to the German text of Kant are from *Kants Gesammelte Schriften*, Bd. 1–8, Berlin 1902–1938, abbreviated here as *KGS*; page references to the *Critique of Pure Reason* are to the 1st = A and 2nd = B editions).

2. *Ibid.*, pp. 108 (*KGS*, Bd. 4, p. 440).

3. 'What is Enlightenment?' in *Kant on History* (Indianapolis, Indiana 1963) p. 10 (*Beantwortung der Frage*: *Was ist Aufklärung? KGS*, Bd. 8, p. 43).

4. Notre Dame, Indiana 1981.

5. For instance, James Collins *The Emergence of Philosophy of Religion* (New Haven, Connecticut 1967); Michel Despland *Kant on History and Religion* (Montreal 1973); Philip Rossi 'Moral Autonomy, Divine Transcendence and Human Destiny' *The Thomist* 46 (1982) 441–458; Allen W. Wood *Kant's Moral Religion*, (Ithaca, New York 1970); Yirmiahu Yovel, *Kant and the Philosophy of History*, (Princeton, New Jersey 1980).

6. *The Sovereignty of Good*, (New York 1971) p. 80.

7. *loc. cit.*

8. See Stanley Hauerwas *A Community of Character*, (Notre Dame, Indiana 1981).

9. *After Virtue*, p. 59.

10. *The Company of Strangers*, (New York 1981) p. 36.

11. *loc. cit.*

12. *Groundwork* pp. 100–101 (*KGS*, Bd. 4, pp. 433–434).

13. Trans. T. H. Greene and H. H. Hudson, New York[2] 1960, pp. 85–114 (*Religion innerhalb der Grenzen der blossen Vernunft*, *KGS*, Bd. 6, pp. 93–124).

14. *Critique of Pure Reason*, trans. N. K. Smith, New York 1929, A 805/ B 833 (*Kritik der reinen Vernunft*, *KGS*, Bd. 3–4).

15. Trans. L. W. Beck, Indianapolis, Indiana 1958, p. 123 (*Kritik der praktischen Vernunft*, *KGS*, Bd. 5, p. 119).

16. The work cited in note 15, p. 89 (*KGS*, Bd. 6, p. 97).

17. *Ibid.*, pp. 88–93 (*KGS*, Bd. 6, pp. 95–102).

18. For development of this point, see Philip Rossi 'Kant's Doctrine of Hope: Reason's Interest and the Things of Faith' *The New Scholasticism* 52 (1982) 228–238.

Konrad Hilpert

The Theological Critique of 'Autonomy'

THE IDEA of autonomy entered theology by a somewhat roundabout route, thus creating difficulties for its 'secondary' host. For it obliged theology to take account of autonomy's original context in philosophy and ethics. 'Autonomy' is associated above all with the name and influence of Kant. Originally it was a term in politics and jurisprudence; indeed it has remained so, and has entered into the terminology of many of the anthropological sciences. It was adopted into philosophical ethics primarily because it was able to express the dual thrust of the Kantian approach—i.e., the rational will as the highest law of morality, and the abandonment of the moral principles of former times, based on results, inclination or authority—and also because it could keep at bay the mistaken conclusion, so readily made, that this approach exposed morality to arbitrary subjectivism.

1. FIVE WAYS IN WHICH 'AUTONOMY' WAS TAKEN UP BY THEOLOGY

Theology reacted to the philosophical notion of autonomy in very diverse ways. In part this was due to the considerable development, change of emphasis and reinterpretation experienced by the concept in the course of the history of thought in modern times.[1] Much more significant, however, was the way a particular theological approach saw itself in relation to contemporary post-Christian society and to its own historical inheritance.

(a) All references to the idea of autonomy in the traditional textbooks of moral theology up to the time of Vatican II are decidedly negative in tone. The context is almost exclusively defensive. To be 'autonomous' is to be no longer 'Catholic'. Characteristic of this kind of apologetics is V. Cathrein's assertion that Kantian autonomy destroys the true moral order because it wrenches man from his proper place.[2] Autonomous morality appears to be the enemy of Christian morality. This view does not refer initially to Kant, of course, but to the liberalist and positivist circles who were working for a complete separation of Church and State, in particular in the matter of education. They simply used Kant as their prime witness in arguing that there could be a 'purely secular' moral order. Most moral theologians at the time supported the view that, deprived of a theistic foundation and the link with Christian revelation, the basis of morality supporting society would gradually collapse—a view still current half a century later, even among theologians committed to internal Church renewal. Some even went so far as to say that the catastrophe of European civilisation, manifested in despotism and the World Wars,

9

was ultimately the result of the middle-class notion of the autonomous subject autonomously shaping his own existence. Thus in 1950 R. Guardini wrote, 'all those inconceivable systems of degradation and destruction' of recent decades 'cannot simply be attributed to the perversity of individuals or small groups; they are the fruit of corruptions and poisons which have long been at work. Things such as moral norms, personal responsibility, honour, the vigilant conscience, do not vanish overnight from the face of society unless they have been emptied of value long ago'.[3] And in Guardini's view this devaluation was the result of the 'blind faith of rebellious autonomism'.[4]

(b) Whereas the above approach to autonomy sees it as a threat, as something incompatible with theology's understanding of itself, there is a second approach which is quite contrary. Here, the modern concept of autonomy is fully acknowledged and interpreted as the actual implementation of Christian theology's ultimate goal. 'Autonomy' here is a term which *unites* Christian morality and modern ethics (i.e., the way modern life sees itself). However, it would be incorrect simply to equate the two: what is involved is in fact the awareness of a third and quite different dimension, namely that in which—to use P. Tillich's metaphor—'autonomy enters into itself so profoundly that it eventually points beyond itself'.[5] This new autonomy, revealed in the very depths of itself, acquires a new name: theonomy. On the one hand 'theonomy' is far beyond an autonomy merely left to its own devices, which easily falls prey to inhuman exploitation. On the other it is opposed to heteronomy, 'such as that found in the Catholic idea of authority, which rejects autonomy'.[6] Despite this distinction between autonomy and theonomy, the two are inseparable, to such an extent that, wherever autonomous culture finds itself opposed to religion, it is automatically in the right.[7] Culture is always religious, not in intention but in substance.[8] Wherever a blind autonomy emerges, unaware of its own depths, it is always simply a reaction to a religion which has lost sight of God but is still trying to keep society in heteronomous dependence on itself.[9] It follows that there must not be a theological ethics *alongside* autonomous philosophical ethics.[10] The most important task for theological ethics is to demonstrate its unity with philosophical ethics, to renounce its independence and to devote itself, within the context of a 'theology of culture' encompassing all fields, to tracing the elements of the unconditional in the given conditional world.

(c) These are only the two most prominent theological reactions to 'autonomy'. In spite of their opposed views, they are united in being deeply marked by their interest in issues of culture and society. This forms a link with the use made by Vatican II of the concept of 'autonomy', although here the aim is different again: it is concerned neither with defensive measures nor with establishing identity, but with delineating the respective areas of competence of theological and pastoral skills on the one hand and earthly structures on the other, against the background of the *skandalon* of the gap between culture and the Church. In the first place this is an internal debate in which the Church is quite consciously coming to grips with the fact that it is no longer omnicompetent. But at the same time it involves a profession of faith, and to that extent is addressed to those 'outside', letting 'the modern world' know that it is ready and willing to become involved in dialogue on a partnership basis. Now it seems possible to seek truth together, even in the very practical terms which are so necessary if the antinomies of modern culture are to be overcome. This cannot be achieved by stubborn self-assertion, nor by indifference to what is distinctive in one's own approach, but only as a result of peaceful and patient effort, undertaken in dialogue. It may be just as necessary for us to make corrections in our tradition as it is for others to advance from a purely intramundane humanitarianism. Thus the Council deplores 'certain attitudes (not unknown among Christians) deriving from a shortsighted view of the rightful autonomy of science', but adds: 'However, if by the term "the autonomy of earthly affairs" is meant that material being does not depend on God and that man can use it as if it had no relation to its creator, then the falsity of such a claim will be obvious to anyone who believes in God'.[11]

(d) This extensive use of the notion of 'autonomy' with regard to the various cultural disciplines was taken up by the postconciliar debate in moral theology. Attempts were made to translate it into the terms of a theological ethics—which the Pastoral Constitution had not mentioned as such. This was done most forcibly by A. Auer in his book *Autonome Moral und christlicher Glaube*, published in 1971. His fundamental conviction is that 'reality contains an inherent truth or rationality, and that . . . it can be recognised, expressed, and communicated, at least to the extent demanded by human action . . . Ethical awareness is made possible thus: the insights of the human and social sciences into the factors involved in human action are taken together with the insights of philosophical anthropology into the meaning of human existence; this brings to light the demands and necessities implied by successful human existence and these are translated into the language of ethical obligation'.[12] Here human reason is credited with the competence to discover concrete ethical guidelines for action in the world. The Church's *magisterium* is still seen as having a particular task of ratification, criticism and stimulation, but at the same time the autonomous moral sense is able in principle to identify certain phenomena as springing from an illegitimate autonomy.[13] In this new scheme, the notion of autonomy is applied primarily for the purposes of *integration*. Theological ethics has an undisputed role as an independent discipline (contrary to Tillich's view) and is concerned to demonstrate its autonomy within the perspective of the Christian message, 'so that contemporary man may have access' to its theological truth.[14]

(e) Auer sees a basis for this approach in, among other things, the attempts made by individual moral theologians at the turn of the eighteenth and beginning of the nineteenth centuries. For the negative view of 'autonomy' (see a above) had not always been so entrenched. True, we meet with such views even in the Enlightenment itself, but the other voices were there too, until Neo-Scholasticism was formally embraced. Theologians such as S. Mutschelle (1749–1800) and J. Geishüttner (1763–1805) concerned themselves expressly with Kant's ethics of autonomy, convinced that it 'accords with the teaching of Christ and with pure Christian virtue'.[15] By adopting the idea of autonomy they hoped to overcome the weakness of the moral theology they had inherited, above all the lack of a speculative basis and a fully systematic treatment, and its casuistic approach. 'Autonomy' is now being used to carry out structural and material *repairs to the theory*, so that the latter can better acquit itself at the bar of critical reason. There is no danger in this, for reason itself is held to be 'God's word',[16] and, conversely, positive revelation only has a ratifying and anticipatory function. There is no question here of revelation going beyond this role; it cannot exercise Auer's 'criticising' function. Moreover, the view of the Enlightenment theologians differs from Auer's 'integrative' view of autonomy in that they absolutely reject the possibility of determining ethical imperatives empirically, by the so-called human sciences; it is a matter for pure reason alone.

2. AUTONOMY AS A PRACTICAL HERMENEUTICAL CATEGORY OF THE MODERN AGE AND MODERN ETHICS

Wherever it occurs in theology, the notion of autonomy is given a definite positive or negative evaluation. But in each case, irrespective of the particular stance, theology's aim is always the same, namely, to determine the relationship between Christian faith or Christian ethics and contemporary society. In each case, moreover, the topics raised are the same: theology's claim to be speaking of revealed matters, the scope of human reason, and, above all, freedom in the sense of the individual subject's free-standing ethical competence. These, however, are plainly the topics raised by the Enlightenment, topics which not only make their mark on philosophical ethics, metaphysics, epistemology and the whole theoretical field, but go on to play a fundamental part in shaping the political, economic and cultural context. Thus we see that the problems of the Enlightenment are thoroughly contemporary. Theology's response to 'autonomy' confirms something that the history of the concept itself can only suggest: for theologico-ethical reflection, 'autonomy' is a specific indicator, a *comprehensive interpretative category of modern philosophical ethics*. This does not rule out the possibility of tracing the historical origins of its concepts and problems further back, before modern times, in order to explain, confirm, or even to criticise them; but it does mean that we cannot have direct recourse to a supposedly normative ethics of the Middle Ages or of Christian antiquity (which was equally 'autonomous', as we can see in retrospect). To do so would be to confuse the basic issue.

With regard to the particular task of determining the place of Christian ethics in modern society, the five typical reactions we have described have something else in common: theology's involvement with the notion of autonomy, from the very first reference right up to the present day, has been connected with its *own diagnosis of an internal crisis*. Even where we seem to witness the self-confident dismissal of opponents, it is motivated by the awareness of inner (and not merely outer) vulnerability. Neo-Scholastic apologists may admit that certain areas call for reform, such as the excessively juridical approach, casuistics, the predominance of the doctrine of sin, the slowness to tackle problems of social ethics. But in the last two decades it is the 'crisis of morality' approach which more clearly addresses the change in social mores and the discrepancy between them and the values put forward by the Church and theology—clearly and characteristically seen in the reactions to the encyclical *Humanae vitae*. Moral theology is coming under increasing pressure from new ethical questions arising from technological progress. A large proportion of these problems affects humanity as a whole, and, as yet, there is no answering sense of responsibility on a global scale. Thus it is all the more urgent for those concerned with theological ethics to work together with all who are anxious about the future of human society—Christians, those of other faiths and those of none—in the search for solutions. Such a task, however, requires a common basis, which presents itself in the form of rational argument.

3. THE CLOSENESS OF CHRISTIAN ETHICS AND MODERN PRACTICAL REASON, AND THE DISTANCE BETWEEN THEM[17]

There is no disagreement that the Christian message of salvation in Jesus Christ, with the moral conduct which is involved in following him, *must be responsibly articulated under modern conditions*. Even if modern philosophy and ethics proved to be opposed to a religiously grounded moral teaching, and thus had to be regarded by theology as irreconcilable with its own view of itself, they would still have much to say about the climate of thought in which a large part of modern society thinks and acts, seeks and establishes truth, ratifies conviction and consent, justifies and acknowledges moral claims. The new approach in moral theology has declared itself by taking 'autonomy' as its watchword and its methodological principle; it is the legitimate task of this approach to appraise the present situation and to face its critical demands and alternative perspectives in a self-critical spirit, without immediately branding them as 'delusion' or 'rejection'. Defensive measures alone will not solve the precarious situation of the Christian ethos in modern times. A moral theology which was satisfied with defence would be grossly oversimplifying things.

Another reason why theology cannot simply dismiss 'autonomy' as suspect is this: its view of man, the world, history and obligation can be shown to be related, in origin and in fact, to the *Christian idea of creatureliness*. Man, freely determining himself, and the world which follows the laws of its nature, both owe their being to God. They are in no way a threat to his freedom, which upholds the whole of reality. Certainly we have to ask at this point whether, once it has broken loose from its origin and guarantor (or even simply lost the awareness of this relation), this creaturely freedom may not adopt inhuman forms. If then, quite properly, we interpret modern society using the concept of autonomy, we once again encounter the fundamental question put to Christianity by modern times, as formulated by Lessing: how can its truth be based on historical events and at the same time have eternal significance? But now, as it were from the other side of the 'terrible, wide ditch', the question rebounds on its originator: Does what has developed historically and concretely from the idea of pure rationality not threaten its own content in so far as it is held to be eternal and above history? Without wishing to minimise the enormous improvements, which no one would want to do without, we would be slow to answer No to this question, in view of our experience of the dark side of modern progress and our growing awareness of it. Theology has to face the question, in a nutshell, whether it is not part of man's creatureliness to reach beyond his freedom.

A transcendence of this kind on man's part is central to the Christian faith; it has a basis in salvation history. It is expressed most signally in the idea of *human and personal dignity*. This implies that every man has intrinsic value and a claim to be respected, and that this cannot be relativised by any other considerations, not even by ethical performance. It exercises a normative function in placing other people's existence (and also one's own existence) outside the ambit of one's own freedom. Of course, we can 'guarantee' human dignity even without explicitly acknowledging it, but only provided the transcendental dimension is at least kept open (as in a kind of negative anthropology). But this is a borderline case, and its plausibility depends on the presence of a religious rationale or on concrete historical experience of the violation of man's dignity.

In terms of salvation history, man's dignity is also based on the *eschatological hope*. In this perspective every individual has his place, and today's achievements are rescued from sinking into oblivion; furthermore, everything evil, everything which isolates and destroys, will finally be nullified. This also means that human life and human intercourse has not yet reached its goal. Freedom, in the sense of modern 'autonomy', only aims at the individual's self-fulfilment; but unless it is linked to the fostering of community it is bound to lead to disappointments. The idea of autonomy, in itself, cannot provide freedom with any principle for building up the *community* and protecting the weaker members. *Reason too, as the basis for agreement, is affected* by this general proviso. While it is true that knowledge of the truth is possible, in principle, even now, prior to the fulfilment of the *eschaton* (see Rom. 1:19ff.; 2:14ff.), it is doubtful whether it is ever attained. References to a time when the law of God will be written on men's hearts, making all external teaching superfluous (Jer. 31:33f.), are in the realm of promise, which has begun to be fulfilled in Jesus. They are not a description of present reality. We owe a great deal to the doctrine of the natural moral law, for the way in which it has protected and nurtured the idea that certain fundamental values can be shared by the most diverse people and groups. Yet, now more than ever, we know that this kind of universality does not mean that things are so in fact. It is a construct; theologically speaking it is an eschatological assumption, normative in that it commits Christians to work towards this universality and, in their own community, to be a sign of it. The 'reason' invoked by theologically autonomous morality is not simply identical with the insight to which faith lays claim; moreover, in its socio-historical reality it manifests internal disunity. Naturally, a plurality of approaches, all claiming the title 'reason', conflicts with the goal of universality; but theology must reckon with it. Thus, while moral theology must by no means abandon itself to irrationality or to a positivistic ethics of 'decision', it need not feel obliged to stigmatise as 'irrational' those deviant value-systems which trumpet their own reasonability, nor to take over and exploit such systems as fit in with its own tradition. The former is arrogant, while the latter often gives the impression of being purely pragmatic, and puts in question the whole purpose of theological reflection on human activity. The recognition of plurality does not mean that the person who distances himself from the Christian faith may not arrive at the same ethical conclusions as the believer; but it does mean that, confronted with competing value-systems, theological ethics does not *have* to prove the exclusive rationality of its own approach. Otherwise theology is inclined to start making normative definitions as to what is rational, or to be too quick to canonise its own inherited tradition. Communicability is something we must search for and take pains over; we must not imagine that it is already there.

Finally, theologically speaking, man is involved in transcendence because he is *in a soteriological relation to Jesus*. Ethically he has in Jesus a pattern and an example, showing him how it is possible to live in freedom *and* solidarity, reason *and* hope. It is clear that a life of this kind does not exclude the *cross*, the *skandalon*—and this implies criticism of those who see freedom only in terms of individual happiness or in the satisfaction of group interests. It follows that if Christian ethics is to prove its value in today's world, it must be in touch with that experiential history which began with and in Jesus, and in touch with the community of those who, in their ethos, manifest the influence of that history. Here and there such an approach is bound to lead to confrontation with what can seem rational from an autonomous point of view. Today this kind of difficulty is becoming more evident in the differing stances on abortion and euthanasia, and in the existence of relationships and communities which reject marriage. We are bound to do all in our power to encourage modern ethics and Christian morality to leave behind their defensive positions and enter into a fruitful encounter; but there is no guarantee that, at the end of the day, all tension between them will have been eliminated.

Translated by Graham Harrison

Notes

1. I have tried to demonstrate this development by reference to significant philosophico-ethical ideas in my book *Ethik und Rationalität* (Düsseldorf 1980). The models presented in the book do not, however, claim to be exhaustive, nor am I suggesting that the development is an inevitable process.

2. *Moralphilosophie* vol. 1 (Freiburg ²1904) p. 216.

3. *Das Ende der Neuzeit* (Basle 1950) p. 103, see pp. 70f., 72f., 93–105, 114f., 120, 124f. Guardini was not using this critique for the ends of a cultural 'Restoration': he argued that a structurally new period had dawned, the beginnings of which were already observable.

4. *Ibid.* p. 101, and see pp. 120–124.

5. 'Theonomie' *RGG* VI (2nd ed.) p. 1128.

6. *Ibid.*

7. Tillich 'Die Überwindung des Religionsbegriffs in der Religionsphilosophie', *Gesammelte Werke* I (Stuttgart 1959) p. 387.

8. *Idem* 'Religionsphilosophie', *Gesammelte Werke* I p. 386f.; see p. 330f.

9. See the same author 'Die Überwindung', *Gesammelte Werke* I p. 386f.; 'Das System der Wissenschaften nach Gegenständen und Methoden', pp. 272f., 274–276; 'Religionsphilosophie', pp. 330f.

10. *Idem* 'Über die Idee einer Theologie der Kultur', *Gesammelte Werke* IX (Stuttgart 1967) pp. 15–19, 25; 'Das System der Wissenschaften' *Gesammelte Werke* I pp. 273f.

11. *Gaudium et spes* no. 36; see nos 41 and 55f.: *Vatican Council II, The Conciliar and Post Conciliar Documents*, ed. A. Flannery (Dublin 1975).

12. A. Auer 'Zur Rezeption der Autonomie-Vorstellung durch die katholisch-theologische Ethik' in *Theol. Quartalschrift* 161 (1981) p. 4f.

13. In this connection Auer speaks of 'absolute autonomy' or 'radically autonomistic morality'.

14. Auer, the work cited in note 12, p. 4, and see p. 6.

15. Mutschelle *Vermischte Schriften oder philosophische Gedanken und Abhandlungen* I (Munich ²1799) p. 216.

16. *Idem* IV, pp. 127–146.

17. We have approached this relationship from the point of view of theology. Of course it could have been approached from the standpoint of philosophical ethics. In the latter case the primary question would be how far a theological ethics which is committed to the idea of autonomy is able to deal with the problems raised by modern ethics. See my book *Ethik und Rationalität* (note 1 above) pp. 455–530.

Bernard Quelquejeu

Ethical Autonomy and the Question of God

WHEN ONE attempts to discern, in as integrated an overall view as possible, the complex chain of intellectual, moral, economic and political upheavals which have finally produced the 'modern world', one cannt fail to be struck by the emergence of new experiences of reality, which involve new ethical attitudes and previously unknown normative evaluations. Amongst the latter, the following may be listed as examples: man's will to achieve technical domination over nature, both the external world of nature and his own nature, which includes the determination to make use of his reason in every area of life; the will to attain unconditional freedom, involving the universal aspiration to self-determination; man's fundamental will relating to political equality, understood in its widest sense as the equality of the conditions which have a determining effect on his existence in the world; a lively awareness of the historical mutability of human existence and of all its categories, an awareness which is often linked to an implicit or explicit belief in progress.[1]

These new experiences of reality, rich in hitherto unknown ethical and normative attitudes, constitute an anthropological consciousness in which the key words are, no doubt, the demand for *liberty* and the recognition by man of his own *dignity*. At the heart of the great variety of claims which are expressed everywhere in the form of human rights, it is not difficult to identify straight away demands for *liberty*, which can be analysed as rights to self-determination, whether on the individual level or on the level of responsible participation in the decisions and the destiny of the community. There must be no misconception in this respect: it is not first of all subjective free will which originally inspires this new anthropological viewpoint; it is far more accurate to say that this liberty is the result of man's reasonable and responsible autonomy. Thus the essential common element of these diverse claims clearly seems to consist in the demand for 'autonomy', the individual making his own laws. Conceived in ethical and political terms, the autonomy which is in question here governs a constantly evolving man considered as a free subject in a free society.

It is precisely on the basis of this responsible liberty, the essential principle of ethical autonomy, that modern man attributes to himself a *dignity* which is inalienable and inviolable. It should no doubt be noted that this dignity will be differently understood in accordance with the viewpoint of the various religions or the great ideologies (image of God, child of God, rational animal, autonomous personality, nexus of social

16

relationships, etc.). This diversity will nevertheless express the common and immutable realisation that in this dignity there is encountered an absolute value which it is no longer permissible to relativise. In this dignity resides the immediate basis of all the ethical and political evaluations, all the normative systems on which modern societies are founded.

The preceding articles have examined the cultural and political sources of the concept of *autonomy*, understood in this sense as the basis of the inviolable dignity of man and of his fundamental demand for liberty. They have examined how, in Christianity, it has been possible for this concept to be received by theologians with reactions ranging from enthusiastic support to clear rejection, and on occasion critical discernment. The purpose of this present contribution is to examine the extent to which 'liberty is a possibility of conceiving God', in H. Krings's formula. In other words, to seek to discern what has become of the traditional 'question of God' in a world which has emerged from the Enlightenment and the process of secularisation and which claims as its own the anthropological perspective which we have just referred to, and no longer accepts, collectively at least, any other ethic than that of autonomy.

Rather than confining ourselves to general considerations, which are always inadequate in brief articles, we considered it preferable to take as points of reference certain attempts which have effectively been made by philosophers to put the question of God in this context. Because of our own personal preferences and competence, and also since it seems to be too little known to many readers of this journal, we have chosen to restrict ourselves to a line of thinkers habitually referred to as those associated with 'philosophies of reflection'. Since historically the latter originated in Kant's meditation on God and in the intellectual and moral revolution which it brought about in that sphere, it is indispensable to begin by summarising briefly the 'moral proof' of God according to Kant.

1. MORAL AUTONOMY AND THE RELIGIOUS QUESTION ACCORDING TO KANT

Before Kant, the problem of morality had most frequently been approached by the ancient philosophers as that of the definition of the 'sovereign good', established in relation to the theological question. Viewing the problem in the light of the central preoccupation of his philosophy—which is to examine before the bar of reason the legitimate use of our faculties—Kant displaced it from its traditional position and showed that the real problem for philosophical reason could not consist in determining what is in itself the 'sovereign good', but in determining what is the nature of the good *action*, that which is posited by a good *will*. The analysis of the good will[2] allows it to be demonstrated that the only definable idea of an absolute good of the will is that of an unconditional disposition of the will, i.e. of the relationship which it posits between itself and the moral law. Absolute good lies in a will which wishes to act only through pure 'respect' for the moral law.

This displacement of the moral question has had as its principal consequence the recognition of the principle of the *autonomy* of the will, in total opposition to all forms of heteronomy. Compared with all those doctrines which founded the moral order on the existence of a Supreme Legislator, there is no exaggeration in speaking of a revolution in moral philosophy. What must be emphasised at this point are the consequences of this revolution for the way in which the question of God is posed.

Kant's analysis in the Dialectic of the *Critique of Practical Reason* concerning the idea of the sovereign good results in the conclusion that it is unreasonable to include in one single idea that good which is the goal of the sensibility, which is happiness, and that good of the will which is the pure disposition to obey the moral law through respect for it. But if it is not possible to depart, however little, from that principle of the autonomy of the free will, it does not follow as a consequence—let us admire the rigour of the Kantian meditation—that the 'prospect' of happiness should have no place in the idea of the sovereign good, as the 'entire object'[3] of the will. Why?

Because we cannot prevent ourselves from thinking that it is just that the man who acts morally should receive the reward of his virtue in the form of happiness. This is a requirement which is just and reasonable: it is not only, nor primarily, a desire of the sensibility, which would incline us to believe that happiness should be realised for us; it is, above all, a judgment enounced by reason, and required by it. In the act by which, in obedience to the moral law, I do my duty, there is implied, according to Kant, not only the intellectual conviction of the obligation of duty, but also the belief that the natural order is not contrary to that duty. Would not duty be a senseless illusion if we were unable to believe that our present state is not definitive, that holiness itself (the constant disposition to pure reverence for the moral law) is not a state which is against nature?

It is therefore a meaningful requirement, formulated by reason and recognised from the beginning as implied in the idea of the sovereign good, that we should be able to conceive—without, moreover, knowing how it will be possible—that we have before us the prospect of an infinite development of our morality, and that in the future there will be a just correlation between morality and happiness. The first part of this requirement produces in us the rational belief—not in the form of speculative knowledge but of practical necessity—in the immortality of the soul; the second, the rational belief in the existence of God. Both are thus implied in the moral act.

Certainly we cannot visualise the possibility of this harmony between virtue and happiness being realised solely by the processes of nature as we know it; we can no more easily believe that our will can, simply by its own endeavours, unite happiness and virtue. But the voluntary act would remain meaningless if we were unable to believe that God, the intelligent Cause and holy Will, has organised the tangible world in such a way as to make possible within it the infinite development of morality and grants the just reward of virtue in the form of happiness. To believe in the existence of God, who has prepared the 'realm of ends', in Kant's words, or the 'kingdom of God', in Christian terms, is not a duty, nor even a simple 'need'. It is a rational requirement, a 'belief' for practical reason, a postulate of which the negation would entail as a consequence the absurdity of human action.

Posing the question of God in such a way distinguishes Kant's thought from that of all previous philosophers—except perhaps for Rousseau. Its originality lies in the fact that it depends on the evidence of the moral consciousness, by which we attain the absolute. God exists because we know that duty exists: and that is something which no speculative sceptic can doubt. It is in vain that we seek for God outside ourselves if we have not first discovered him within us, in the heart of that pre-existing and indestructible certainty, which can and must survive the ruin of our knowledge and convictions, whether concrete or abstract.

Before Kant, religions and philosophies had founded the reality and the necessity of the moral law on the prerequisite of the existence of God. Kant, concerned to ensure the autonomy of ethics, reverses the terms of this proposition. It is essential to appreciate the full extent of this revolution. For him—he believes moreover that he is thus expressing the true meaning of the Christian religion—there can be no question of making the moral law dependent on a Supreme Legislator. The law is not worthy of respect because a God is supposed to have established it. It is absolutely worthy of respect because we first discover it within ourselves, we are certain of it through a sort of rational revelation—and it is only by reflecting on this law and the conditions necessary for it to be respected that we subsequently attain to the idea of its Author. Any other source of its obligatory nature would make the moral law null and void in its essential principle, by founding it on a destructive heteronomy. God cannot be attained as the necessary cause of the moral law, since that law cannot have any principle outside the will itself, and that will is autonomous. In the thought of the founder of the ethic of autonomy, God can be attained—by a reflective detour involving the idea of an infinite moral progression of which the certainty is inseparable from the moral act—only as the author of the laws of nature which are compatible with the existence of the moral being,—in short, as the moral legislator of nature. We cannot 'demonstrate' the existence of God: but when we aspire towards the good with the full liberty of our nature, it is impossible for us not to affirm the reality of that good, and therefore the immortality of the soul and the existence of God.

It is Kant's glorious achievement to have detached the question of God from the realm of pure speculation and established it at the heart of free human action. It is by an absolute act of freedom that one discovers (posits) the reality of the absolute. Before seeking it we have already, in some sense, found it. To make this implicit reality explicit a 'reflection' is needed, a reflective act which was to be the object of prolonged examination by a whole series of systems of thought which may legitimately be called *reflective philosophies*. Before examining in broad outline one or another of those which have applied themselves to the question of God, thus prolonging the investigation of the possibility of the affirmation of God, on the basis of the autonomy of ethics, it is worth sketching briefly the common inspiration and the tradition of these philosophies of reflection.

2. THE TRADITION OF THE REFLECTIVE PHILOSOPHIES

The true point of departure which influences, in various ways, these different philosophies is obviously the Cartesian *cogito*, 'the irrefutable *cogito*'.[4] If I doubt everything, I do not doubt that I doubt. This is an essential stage: the world which I conceive is still in doubt, whereas my thought is no longer so. This first certainly immediately implies another: this subject, this I to which thought spontaneously relates, is not the empirical, psychological consciousness, still linked to the objects in the world, which still remains in doubt. It was soon to be called 'transcendental', this thinking consciousness, the product of methodical doubt, and 'reflective analysis'[5] the method which attempts to develop the results of this establishing of the indubitable. 'It is good that I should pause for a while here', said Descartes. One may approve his decision, for what is involved is the experience of the *mind* (*esprit*). An attempt has been made to define it as 'the operative unity of a relationship being exercised, interior to itself'.[6] Indeed, it is difficult to conceive of the mind; it is within us only as the principle of action. The action itself may be thought, but not the source of the action. The mind is that by which we know, not that which is known; it is that by which objects exist, it cannot itself be an 'object'. 'The mind', said Lavelle, echoing so many others, 'is not an object which may be seen; it is an *act* which can only be perceived in its actual accomplishment'. One writer[7] has even spoken of an isolation and a despair of the mind, of an irreducible opacity of the mind.

As a technical term, although this still remains very general, we may understand by 'reflection' the initial *act* by which the subject initially constitutes itself and by which it assures itself of its existence, its power, its truth, and subsequently perceives, immanent in its operations, the laws and norms of mental activity in every area. 'What is the quintessential act of the mind, that is to say the one which best lends itself to the reflective experience? One may well hesitate, and, in fact, what differentiates, from the outset, the various reflective philosophies, is their choice of the act to which this first reflection is to be applied. Sometimes it is the act of thinking, judging, affirming, sometimes the creation or the intellection of the sign, sometimes the immediate apperception of the self in the original fact of its own effort'.[8]

Reflective analysis may in fact set out, and has effectively done so, in two principal and different directions, which are already implied in the Cartesian *cogito*. Firstly, it may apply itself to the discovery, in the operations of the knowing subject, of the conditions which make possible genuine experience. This was to be the way inaugurated by Kant and later followed by J. Lagneau, J. Lachelier, L. Brunschvicg, P. Lachièze-Rey. . . . Next, it may, without in any way denying the transcendental consciousness, choose to explore more deeply or to liberate the intimate nature of the self by appropriating those more concrete experiences with which the destiny of the self is essentially linked. This was to be the Biranian tendency in reflective philosophy. Opened up by *Maine de Biran*, in the analysis of the 'original fact' of the effort made by the self, of the immediate consciousness of a relationship between an act of the subject and the resistance which it encounters, this line of thought was to be developed by thinkers such as G. Madinier, P. Ricoeur, J. Nabert. One must immediately emphasise the manifestly complementary nature of these two tendencies in reflective analysis, the first applied on the level of knowing, the second rather on the level of action. 'It was necessary', J. Nabert judiciously adds, 'that a critical theory of knowledge should have particularly emphasised in the "I think" its function of objectivity and truth, in order to avoid the risk of researches immediately concerned with the concrete forms of inner experience making concessions to a sterile irrationalism'.[9]

The most illustrious representative of the Biranian tendency is Jean Nabert. In his thesis of 1924, *L'Expérience intérieure de la liberté*, he has shown that the opposition between nature and freedom changes its meaning when freedom is no longer sought either in an intemporal causality which transcends the causality which exists in the world of phenomena, or in the gaps in the theories of determinism, or in the imitation of an intelligible order opposed to the vicissitudes of the tangible world, but in the progress of an *inner experience* which is nothing less than a ceaseless reflective scrutiny by the self of its own actions, in order to verify the nuances and the quality of a 'causality of the mind' which does not emerge immediately, in its purity, from our passions and instinct (*ibid.*) Nabert subsequently devoted himself, still with the same rigorous fidelity to the reflective method, to the fundamental questions of a moral philosophy.[10] In place of a morality of which the inefficacity is all too obvious so long as it limits itself to opposing the dignity of duty to everything which proceeds from 'nature', reflection introduces the intensification of an experience which discovers in human tendencies and desires an aspiration which a concrete ethical system may put in the service of the 'desire to be'. For the idea of an evil which is solely attributable to the finite nature of creatures, to their limitations, to the privations which they endure, reflective experience substitutes the analysis of an evil which has its roots in the human heart, in its solitude, its indifference to others and of which the 'unjustifiable' character may, if necessary, be recognised without destroying the effort to reappropriate the self and without compromising the unending promotion of values. Having thus respected the specific character of an ethic of autonomy, Nabert finally turned to the subject of the affirmation of the divine.[11] However, before sketching the main outlines of his reflection on God, a brief digression is necessary. . . .

3. THE 'PROOF OF GOD' ACCORDING TO LANGUAGE: THE *COURS SUR DIEU*[12]

It is thanks to the discoveries of reflective analysis and following in the tradition of its spiritual interiority that J. Lagneau has endeavoured to correct Kant's presentation of the question of God. 'There can be no question (. . .) of replacing Kant's proof by one based on a different principle: (. . .) we can know God only by means of the moral act'; but it is possible 'to make his proof, if not more rigorous, at least more direct' (p. 241). How? Precisely, 'by developing a more exact awareness, through analysis, of the conditions of the proof which is being sought'.

Kant's method suffers, according to Lagneau, from a two-fold defect. On the one hand the rational requirement of an infinite development of morality does not show itself to be an absolutely necessary consequence of the affirmation of the absolute value of the moral law and, in addition, to base this affirmation on a simple requirement will never result in anything more than a precarious belief, which lacks the quality of a necessary truth. Secondly, to deny the requirement of a God who rewards men, ensuring the correlation between virtue and happiness, in no way detracts from the absolute goodness of the moral law. Both of these postulates leave unresolved the question: '*Must* one believe that the nature of things is really arranged by a divine author in accordance with the demands of our own nature?'

It is through a deeper study of autonomous liberty, of the free act of a thinking mind in search of truth, that Lagneau develops further the way opened up by Kant. The demonstration of the necessary existence of God cannot be sufficient for the free mind:[13] the concept of the right to be and of the duty to be is also necessary. 'At the basis of every judgment affirming the truth of something is found the approbation of the mind which considers itself to be free and which affirms itself not merely as existing, as being, but as having a duty to be. The fundamental affirmation of the thinking mind is, not only that something exists (. . .), but that within it something has a duty to be, and that it is only in the conformity between that which is necessarily and that which has a duty to be that we may find the truth of that which is' (p. 244).

One can see in what sense Lagneau interiorises the Kantian proof. The infinite development of morality is not only a postulate which can be challenged, but a useless middle term: the moral act, understood by reflection in its necessary conditions, immediately gives us the relationship of nature to the absolute. Similarly in the case of the concordance of virtue and happiness: 'even if we were not to conceive of the necessity of an exact recompense in the form of happiness, we should nevertheless still be justified in affirming the existence of God' (p. 246). Without having recourse to these 'intermediaries', i.e. to the necessity of attaining God as a principle external to the interiority of the mind, proposing a proof which 'is both moral and metaphysical' (p. 248), Lagneau believes that he has succeeded in 'attaining God directly in the moral act, i.e. (. . .) as the immanent principle of the good' (p. 247). In the long, beautiful pages of the fouth part of the *Cours sur Dieu* he presents the full, carefully-argued development, complete with its premises and its implications, of this 'direct or reflective moral proof of God' (pp. 248–293).

4. THE AFFIRMATION OF GOD IN NABERT'S *LE DÉSIR DE DIEU*[14]

There can be no possibility, in these brief pages, of summing up, even in its main outlines, one of the most outstanding attempts, in our day, to devise a philosophical approach to God which is entirely situated, like Lagneau's, within the context of the acceptance, from the outset, of the ethic of autonomy. At most one may attempt to give some impression of the style of his meditation and also of the experiences or the questions of which it seeks to take account.

There is a very real resemblance between Lagneau and Nabert, which is manifest in a sentence like this: 'the condition for our conceiving God and for our subsequent attaining of God beyond our concept itself, is that he should first have given himself to us in the original desire, or rather in the love which is its basis' (*Cours sur Dieu* p. 248). Despite this, however, there is between them one fundamental difference. In the original desire, in the act by which a consciousness pursues reflectively the comprehension of itself, for Nabert it is the *absence* of God which is given, and for his presence to be able to be given an encounter with a 'witness' to the absolute in history will be necessary. This difference reveals in Nabert's thought a new set of problems which cannot be avoided: that of the relationship with history, that of revelation, that of the testimony given in our history to the absolute.

Nabert's first act[15] had been to dissociate totally the definitions of the 'divine' from any 'being' necessarily possessing divine predicates—a dissociation taken to such lengths that the very idea of 'God' seemed to be afflicted by a definitive agnosticism. This act was, in fact, entirely consonant with the reflective method. 'The understanding objectifies everything to which it applies itself': the idea of a necessary being is only the application of the logic of predication to the fundamental reflective act. Instead of starting from the desire for 'God', a concept void of meaning for the understanding, Nabert's method proposes a reflection on the divine in order to advance towards God rather than starting from him—towards 'a God who is only divine' (p. 330).

What does the 'divine' mean? It cannot be the predicate of a being: it is the character of an act which is inseparable from our reflection motivated by the desire for deliverance and justification. This is why it inspires a normative activity in which reflection makes itself, in some sense, a 'judge of the divine'. What Nadeau calls 'the criteriology of the divine' not only has as its function the pitiless denunciation of the false images or idols of God, but also the enunciation of the criteria for the manifestation of the absolute; that in the name of which a testimony relating to the absolute may be received by a reflective consciousness.

The whole enterprise revolves around this point: What is involved in interpreting a testimony? It is a *twofold* act. It is an act of the historical consciousness, exercising itself on the signs which the absolute gives of itself; it is also an act of the very consciousness of the self, in order to recognise the signs in which it can pursue the reappropriation of itself and the approach to justification. Nabert's response consists in the convergence of these two processes, neither cancelling out the other but, on the contrary, presupposing and criticising it. The signs which 'God' causes to appear in history, thanks to the divine witness, may be the signs in which reflection deepens the progress of the consciousness; inversely, the signs by which a consciousness pursues its desire to be are at the same time the signs given in the testimony of the absolute.

'For the apprehension of the absolute', writes Nabert, 'the nakedness which is essential to the [original] experience and the relationship of the divine to an historical manifestation are complementary. Thanks to the first, the perception of the divine tends to be merged into the progress of reflection simply through the ascesis of the philosophical consciousness; for the latter, the divine introduces itself into history through a testimony of which the consciousness can never exhaust the meaning' (*Le Désir de Dieu* p. 267). What we can and must recognise in such a testimony is that it is the expression of a liberty which we ourselves desire to be.

This circular relationship between two 'centres' of reflection—the criteriology which makes the consciousness the judge of the manifestations of the divine, the hermeneutics of testimony which consents critically to the unpredictability of the event and of the historical revelation—has been tirelessly scrutinised by Nadeau, in search of an affirmation of God which entirely respects the interiority of a spiritual process. The greatness of the thought, unfinished as it was, of Jean Nabert—who never dared to call himself a Christian—consists perhaps, on the basis of the acceptance of the ethical autonomy of man, in having indissolubly linked the return to the origins of reflection, mercilessly critical vigilance in relation to idols and yet, the attentive and finally submissive listening to the revelatory acts of God.

Translated by L. H. Ginn

Notes

1. See J. Schwartländer *Menschenrechte—eine Herausforderung der Kirche* (Mainz 1979).
2. Carried out in *Foundations of the Metaphysic of Morals*.
3. 'Consequently, the sovereign good may well always be the entire object of a practical pure reason, i.e. of a pure will, yet it must nevertheless not be taken to be the *determining principle* of the latter (. . .) This point is important in a matter as delicate as the definition of moral principles, where

even the tiniest misunderstanding corrupts one's intentions' (*Critique of Practical Reason*, Dialectic, ch. 1).

4. E. Borne *Passion de la vérité* (Paris 1962) p. 191.

5. J. Lachelier *Psychologie et métaphysique* (Paris 1912).

6. R. Le Senne *Introduction à la philosophie* (Paris 1939) p. 257.

7. See F. Alquié: unpublished lectures on 'The Essence and Situation of the Mind'.

8. J. Nabert 'Les Philosophies de la réflection' in *L'Encyclopédie Française* (1957), XIX, col. 04–14 to 06–03.

9. *Ibid.* col 06–01.

10. J. Nabert *Eléments pour une éthique* (Paris 1943/1962). *Id. Essai sur le mal* (Paris 1955).

11. J. Nabert *Le Désir de Dieu* (posthumous) (Paris 1966). See *infra* n. 14.

12. This course reproduces a course given at the Lycée Michelet in Paris in 1892–93. It was published in 1925. Our quotations are from the edition in J. Lagneau *Célèbres leçons et fragments* (Paris 1925).

13. 'Thus we must be convinced that it is not a matter of being certain of the existence of God' *Ibid.* p. 249.

14. The thick wad of pages published in 1966 by P. Ricoeur and P. Levert referred to in note 11, represents an unfinished book with a problematical plan, repeated versions etc. See P. Ricoeur's Introduction and P. Naulin's study *Le Problème de Dieu dans la philosophie de Nabert* (Faculté de Clermont-Ferrand 1982).

15. Begun in 1959 in the article 'Le Divin et Dieu' in *Les etudes philosophiques* 14 (1959) pp. 321–332.

C

Volker Eid

The Relevance of the Concept of Autonomy for Social Ethics

1. PRELIMINARY REMARKS

IN THE sense of our modern understanding of man the concept 'autonomous morality' denotes a specific mode of interpretation of the phenomenon of morality. It is understood as not only the implementation of normative rules with regard to attitudes and behaviour but as an essential part of the creative shaping of life and the world. In other words, it is a question not just of obedience with regard to ethical norms but also of responsibility for the development and formation of such ethical norms that serve the business of giving life a meaningful shape. It is thus a question of a fundamental anthropological definition of morality and of an epistemological and methodological comprehension of the process of the formation and realisation of ethical norms. This definition explicitly throws into relief man's ability to shape himself on the basis of his experience and perception.[1]

2. MORALITY IN AN ANTHROPOLOGICAL INTERPRETATION

Moral behaviour is generally regarded as characterised by being a response based on free judgment and on freely accepted responsibility to a situation needing improvement. In this it rests on the ethical values and norms existing in the milieu of the person concerned. Someone is regarded as behaving morally if he or she consciously models himself or herself on the current ethical values and norms and realises these in his or her behaviour, and similarly someone is regarded as behaving immorally for going against them. If this definition of morality is given a one-sided interpretation, it is very easy to reach a morality of obedience and implementation that is predominantly oriented towards achievement. In actual practice this kind of morality is widespread, if not predominant. Its central problem is that the abstract grid of the traditional institutionalised system of moral values and norms is imposed on the entire field of moral behaviour. As a result one's actual perception of whatever situation is involved is to a considerable extent reduced to the data of an abstract list of norms. Such diminished perception has the effect of suppressing spontaneous, creative and sensitive responsibility. What to a considerable extent are lacking are the existential surprise and the spontaneity of action of the person who is ethically challenged. And yet it is not an abstract systematic ethic of norms that tells me how I should behave towards my neighbour but this neighbour himself or herself. And while I can in any event make use of the 'information' supplied by existing norms in order to act responsibly I cannot avoid the task of letting my fellow man or woman in his or her actual situation make claims on me.

It is easy to see that already in this kind of quite 'normal' ethically relevant situation 'morality' appears as a creative activity, in other words as a sensitive summing up of a situation, as a creative involvement with one's ethical responsibility and, included in this, as an equally creative involvement with the ethical norms that are important for the particular situation. A morality that leans towards passive obedience does not fully grasp the reality of a situation and thus often does not arrive at correct behaviour. A morality based on creative responsibility, on the other hand, allows itself to be actively determined by the actual situation and then applies the traditional norms in the process of decision and action. This application of ethical norms to the situation that actually exists is a creative activity which draws the general ethical perceptions that are preserved in the norms and are available to the person concerned into the responsible handling of a particular situation. This avoids the atomism of situation ethics, in other words deciding and acting only on an *ad hoc* basis, following one's emotions, and thus often deciding and acting wrongly. But it will also avoid the danger of only understanding and judging the actual situation according to a catalogue of abstract norms.

The creative or rather productive character of morality observed here is characteristic not just of actual behaviour but of morality in general. Morality means the entire structure of the establishment and maintenance of values, of ethical norms, of patterns of behaviour and of forms of life (institutions, roles) that people have worked out for themselves and go on working out, including doing so by fresh departures and by changes. The working out of morality is a part of that process of coming to grips with and mastering his existence that is quite specifically incumbent on man, because without it human existence would remain shapeless and unfruitful.

It is above all the study of human culture that has brought out that man sees himself as the form of life that is not predetermined and established but that must first discover and establish its form of life and its rules of life in all spheres of existence (such as human inter-relationships, marriage and the family, politics, science and scholarship, art, technology, etc.) and must go on re-examining these and developing them further. Man does not have simply a ready-made nature which he need only put into effect. He must first create his own nature, and indeed do so as culture. It is in this sense that existential philosophers, for example Martin Heidegger in *Being and Time*, state that man is the being called to his very own potential of being, that he owes himself the development and realisation of this potential. This obligation that we are able to experience to sound out and complete our own existence signifies a responsibility that is rooted in the very condition of being human. It depends on the individual how his or her life develops, whether it is a success or a partial or total failure. And this existential responsibility is right from the start specifically attached to man: it belongs to what is essentially human. It is the dynamic foundation of the personality (reason, intellect, emotions, needs) and of human solidarity. And it turns out to be the dynamic foundation of the identity that is maintained and built up through all the vicissitudes of life. It is brought to active prominence by the fact that in all ways of life men are concerned about forms of action that meet the all-embracing need to develop life in keeping with its highest possibilities or to stabilise it at moments of crisis and disappointment. The central existential starting-point for morality thus lies in this experience of responsibility for oneself and the way man is referred to his specific ability to give a meaningful shape to his own life, his life with others and his world. Morality is therefore also a decisive criterion for organisation and behaviour in all spheres of life without exception. To this extent it is a constituent bearer of the whole of human culture.

The thesis that morality is autonomous exactly fits the responsible and creative character of the ethical shaping of life that we have described. It throws into relief the fact that people develop and realise their morality productively in all fields of life, that man has an original and specific ability and duty to discover and establish how his life both as an individual and as a member of society can succeed. Hence the concept of freedom means nothing other than the way man is his own point of reference, his genuine responsibility for shaping his own destiny and his right to decide and to act in such matters without extraneous compulsion.

Of course autonomy and freedom can and should be understood not as absolute but as relational data. Man depends on the pattern of his own being—his personality, how he relates to others, his status as a creature, the way he is historically conditioned, etc.—and on his antecedents, the history of his life, his surroundings. He is not self-sufficient. But he can lay claim to freedom from external demands in the fields of life over which he has to decide and in which he can realise himself in his own characteristic individuality.

The thesis of autonomy put forward here is not to be understood as opposed to theism. It can indeed appeal explicitly to the fundamental insight of Judaeo-Christian belief that productive freedom and responsibility for oneself is a specific characteristic of man as created by God. According to the biblical understanding of man we find sketched out in Genesis creation is indeed directed towards and has as its object man's autonomous achievement of culture. And a central place here is occupied by morality. It is in this sense that we need to understand the concept of theonomous autonomy that is used here and there, for example by Franz Böckle. This should mean that human autonomy is founded and structured as such by God's creative will. The concept of autonomy discloses and confirms the realisation that morality is primarily a fundamental creative potential of man and in keeping with this is the creative task of responsibly shaping one's life.

3. THE DISCOVERY AND JUSTIFICATION OF NORMS ACCORDING TO THE CONCEPT OF AUTONOMY[2]

According to the interpretation of morality that has just been sketched out, man's ethical norms are not something he is simply provided with naturally, nor are they revealed to him in a crude sense. Rather he has to shape them for himself. It is up to man whether his life can succeed. Of course every man and woman is by his or her birth placed within a particular culture and society and thereby also in a particular moral order. He or she is therefore provided with ethical norms. But precisely with regard to this fact there is a great difference between regarding and implementing the norms one encounters as timeless elements that are absolutely valid and recognising that they come at the end of a long process of discovery, establishment and further development, including change, and that the process of creative involvement with ethical norms is never finished. It is only in this way that the ethical norms that have been handed down are recognised as an essential component of an ethical concept of life that is shaped, tested and continually changed within a multitude of dimensions. It is recognised as an aid that people create for themselves socially and individually once they have through experience won the conviction that in a typical situation a particular way of acting or behaving is better than others.

According to the concept of autonomy ethical norms depend, with regard to their origination, their maintenance and their alteration from time to time in keeping with their original intention, on the conclusions drawn from experience, on the conclusions drawn from reason, and on responsible decision. These three elements will now be briefly considered.

(a) Experience is at the moment a central concept in many fields of study concerned with human psychology and behaviour.[3] This is clearly because they are all concerned with the question of how we human beings encounter reality. This presupposes that encountering reality is not simply a process of passively reproducing and illustrating something but a grasp of essential data together with their fundamental structure and their mutual relationship and coherence. This is because we must place ourselves in a relationship to the reality we encounter, otherwise it would remain faceless and without history.

But how does it happen that we are aware of our experiences at all, that we are not simply slotted into a structure of perception in which we are influenced by releasing stimuli? It is simply because we follow our innate will to come to grips with the world. This will to grasp and comprehend the world and to shape it is borne by our instinctive dimension but is something more comprehensive than instinctuality: it is an existential interest in developing as a person in the world. Experience is the existential mode in which we come to grips with our world and our surroundings. It is the existential mode in which we come to grips with ourselves in the world. The moral significance of experience consists in the fact that through it we gain an affective and cognitive grasp of the elements and possibilities of our existence, and this on the basis of the fundamental challenge to realise these possibilities in action. We can for example experience the supportive effect other people's trust and good will have. And we can understand from good and bad experiences that in situations where people depend on each other only loyalty and honesty contribute to success in life but that lying and betrayal thwart it.

(b) Reason is the ability to probe and investigate experiences, to structure them, to bring them into relation with each other and to identify them as meaningful or meaningless, as good or bad. It is through our reason that we are able to establish, by means of an ever-new complex process of reflection, what our experiences mean for the implementation of our life and for our action. And we are also able to refer these latter back again to our experiences. All this is not made up of isolated elements that happen to be juxtaposed but is related to the context of our life as individuals and as members of society. It can for example be the case that a particular action at first produces a thoroughly advantageous and agreeable experience—for example, I succeed without any doubts—but then appears as at least doubtful in connection with a second and third relevant experience: I discover that I am living at someone else's expense and that my egoism and my lack of consideration are developing into a negative quality of my own personality. On the basis of this kind of integration of experiences and links between actions reason is able to develop patterns or models of right living and action; and it can among other things formulate these in ethical directions for behaviour, or norms.

It is the business of reason to develop rules of behaviour or norms that take into account as many relevant experiences as possible (with the aim of taking them all into consideration), as many facts as possible of our existence as individuals and as members of society and of our existence in the universe, and to integrate these by making meaningful connections between them.

In this reason proceeds autonomously: despite all its dependence on the facts of our life and our world it is free when it comes to interpretation and integration. But in turn it is only relatively autonomous in that it cannot create but can only realise its own autonomy. This autonomy is given to it along with being a person, being a member of society and living in the world. Hence reason does not act arbitrarily in working out the meaning of ethical norms. It is tied to personality, belonging to society, being historically conditioned, being a creature, in brief to all that makes being human something *a priori* and something that is not at our disposal. This elementary connection also provides the necessary opportunity to examine and criticise reason for its own sake. As historical reason it is of course not free of the risk of ideological delusion. This kind of delusion can be discovered by means of reason's own critical potentiality.

·The rationality of ethical norms gives rise to their communicability. All ethical norms are subject to the proviso that fundamentally they make rational sense and can be fulfilled.

This does not mean postulating that every ethical norm that I recognise must in certain circumstances be recognised by everybody else. Rather it means postulating that, on the basis of becoming aware of the complex of elements on which it is based, a norm can be made recognisably sensible: in other words, that it has not been imposed arbitrarily and irrationally but emerges from the clarity of rational argumentation. (For example, the interpretation of human sexuality that serves to justify particular norms of sexual morality must be capable of rational accomplishment according to the prevailing state of experience and understanding.) There thus arises a further criterion for ethical norms: conditionality. This means that the meaning and validity of a norm always remain dependent on the principal conditions of the situation and experience in the context of which it came into existence.

(c) For general ethical norms to come into existence responsible decision is the final decisive factor. One could occupy oneself in a purely hypothetical manner with many possibly meaningful rules of behaviour applying to all possible fields of life without establishing them. Ethical norms include within themselves not only the rational judgment reached on the basis of experiences that a particular form of behaviour seems to be fitting for man's social constitution, for example, or the dignity of the created world (ecological morality), but also the responsible decision of all those who have based themselves firmly and consciously on them because they recognise fundamental human possibilities in them. This business of deciding for oneself in favour of a particular morality and the norms tied up with it is an act of freedom on the basis of experience and perception which has its place in the development of every individual life. The attainment of maturity is closely connected with it. And the maturity of a group, community or society depends on how its individual members disclose and elucidate the meaning of existing ethical norms in the rational exchange of their experiences both with themselves and with each other; and how they develop norms further by changing, adopting or reshaping them.

The concept of autonomy helps to make clear the specific competence of the mature human being for his or her ethical norms, as well as the way in which general ethical norms can be attained through experience and the integrating process of rational reflection.

4. TWO EXAMPLES

The hermeneutic and methodological significance of the concept of autonomy will now be briefly indicated by means of two examples. In the space available there can of course be no question of a comprehensive presentation, merely the indication of some examples.

(a) Marriage and the family

Marriage and the family are two central forms of life or institutions which are closely related to each other but are characteristically contrasted with one another. In contemporary understanding marriage is the binding, intimate and faithful partnership of man and woman which contains within itself its humanly fulfilling meaning of total love and complementarity and which on the basis of love expresses itself creatively and procreatively. The family is that community of life in which the marriage partners involve themselves as marriage partners and at the same time as father and mother in the partnership with their children and in which the children for their part involve themselves in the partnership with their parents. The family is a prop and aid not just physically and psychologically but also economically. No one will dispute that marriage and the family are of great moral importance as fundamental forms of life and as fundamental goods. But for traditional moral theology, for social ethics and for the teaching of the Church in general there has been and there is a problem that is not easy to solve. Historical and anthropological studies have shown the extent to which these two institutions have changed in the course of human history, and that there have been valid forms of marriage and the family which from our point of view today we would have to judge as in fact more or less immoral: polygamy, families with shifting patterns of sexual partners among the parents, etc. Essentially the problem lies in the fact that the teaching of the Church tends to see marriage and the family as institutions founded by the creator, as elements of human life that are given in advance. This kind of moral teaching by the Church cannot simply take on board without more ado the findings of historical and anthropological research that both institutions are human products and that to some extent they have undergone a considerable change and may well do so again.

Here the concept of autonomy can help, and in this way. Marriage and the family do of course rest on primary human qualities and fundamental needs. But they are not innate forms of life whose inherent rules, and thus ethical norms, need only be obediently followed and adhered to. They are rather products of the creative reason which, on the basis of experience of the primary qualities and needs, produces forms for coming to grips with existence and shaping human life. The co-ordination and integration of the procreation and upbringing of children with the needs for sexual fulfilment, for all-embracing and supportive love, for mutual help in all fields of life, including the economic, for the education of the children, etc., then leads to the institutions that we know as marriage and the family. These institutions are created by men and women and given a meaningful structure with ethical norms that ensure faithfulness, that demand mutual responsibility and care, etc. But these norms have not been arbitrarily imposed but flow from the experience of basic human qualities and needs (including also, for example, the development of the personality in total sexual love), inasmuch as the creative reason takes these experiences up, interprets them, and integrates them into patterns of life.

In this way the concept of autonomy does not contradict the theological insight that man's fundamental qualities and needs are bestowed on him by the creator. But it makes clear that man's responsibility to develop and establish the human possibilities of living together in partnership on the basis of his own creative abilities also represents a gift of the creator which is also a challenge and obligation. The concept of autonomy can adopt the findings about the historical nature and the mutability of marriage and the family and make it clear that the present form of these institutions should not simply be accepted passively but must be actively developed both in general but also above all in each individual marriage and family. Indeed, every marriage and every family depends on the creative and norm-creating abilities of those who form it. Here the concept of autonomy means encouragement for a creative morality. And this is not in general in contradiction to the teaching of the Church that sees in marriage and the family an area where the love of Jesus Christ apprehended in faith is verified.

(b) The problem of violence

The problem of violence can serve as a second example of the way in which, according to the concept of autonomy, ethical insights and norms are worked out and justified. People can quickly agree that the naked use of physical or psychological violence is to be condemned morally. This admittedly rests on the common recognition of the principle that every human being has an inviolable right to unrestricted self-development and to freedom of opinion and of religion as long as this freedom is not abused egocentrically.

Hence many critics would say that there is just no need for the concept of autonomy in order to arrive at acceptable ethical norms, and that the concept of autonomy does not produce any ethical norms that are superior in their content to those already known. In practice this is so. But one must add at once that it is not a question here of demonstrating some exclusive quality on the part of the concept of autonomy but of showing that the development of ethical norms to cover the problem of violence also springs from the autonomous creative power of man's moral competence. This can be demonstrated in something like the following way.

As is well known, man's inbuilt potential for violence continues to play an important role in human society. Force is necessarily exercised in society because society has to be organised and given a meaningful structure, in certain circumstances and situations even against the will of individuals. At the same time there are many experiences of having to endure the superiority of those who happen to be in power and possession, and this in turn clearly means a lessening of other people's opportunities and their oppression. And we can very easily show methodically that in many groups, communities and states there are power-structures which make use of violence. While for example the haves enjoy their privileges the poor are confirmed in their poverty: physical poverty but also intellectual and spiritual poverty, as for example through linguistic deprivation and the lack of opportunities for education and development.

The experience of all that has been sketched out here produces the realisation that on the one hand in every form of society there is the potential for force and thus for violence; and that for the sake of the good of society as a whole this must be applied. On the other hand there is the realisation that the potential for violence tends to fix and establish prevailing injustices and to oppress the underprivileged. In the train of contemporary ideas of freedom the realisations reached by reason have led us to promote every man and woman's equal right of development, and this for the sake of every man and woman's inherent dignity. Nobody must become simply the object of another. And within the framework of the resources that are at the disposal of society as a whole everybody should be guaranteed the possibility of self-development. Oppressive violence is not to be justified morally but to be rejected. But is the use of violence permitted to make the right of the poor and underprivileged to freedom and development prevail? The history of freedom movements, including Christian ones, shows that the path of the use of violence as the power of the powerless is consistently disputed: the path of controlled violence (Martin Luther King) just as much as the path of revolutionary violence (Camillo Torres and others). At the same time we are keenly aware, in the context of the present conflict between West and East, that the strong-arm threat of violence always leads to an escalation of the level of violence and does not help anyone but instead threatens everyone without exception. Hence we recognise from our experience and from the use of our reason that the success of the human enterprise depends decisively on being able to deal in a controlled way with violence. And from this point we can assent to the bias Jesus showed for the poor, for the hungry, and for those who mourn, as he expressed it in the sermon on the mount, and at the same time can equally decisively accept his demand for the controlled doing away with violence in favour of purging out prejudice and relations of hostility. Coping responsibly with violence tries relentlessly to disclose oppressive relationships of violence, to illuminate the causes, and to do away with relationships of hostility.

Here in my view it becomes conclusively clear that the concept of autonomous morality is able to give motivation and impulse to the creative moral power. It is a question of liberating morality from its one-sided character of implementation and obedience and its fixation with norms and to lead it to an ability to decide and to act that is genuinely guided by experience and reason.

5. AUTONOMOUS MORALITY AND CHRISTIAN FAITH

What was brought out in the prolonged debate over what Christian faith means for morality was that faith does not bring with it a specific morality that would not exist without it. Instead it offers a characteristic context of its own within which morality acquires a definite new place, or indeed a specific 'intentionality' of moral action, an unmistakable horizon against which morality can be situated. There is not therefore some specific Christian morality but rather morality in the context of and in connection with the faith.

This rather cognitive relationship between faith and morality can in my view be filled out existentially. As a responsible creative shaping of existence morality needs a fundamental decision with regard to appraising and evaluating the reality of the world and of life. This is not itself morality but provides its foundation and presupposition. Taking a stand with regard to the world and life as a whole is a consequence of the urgent need to enquire after an aboriginal and persistent truth on which man can rely in the fragmentariness of his efforts and patterns of living. In these, and especially in his efforts to work out his morality, he is aiming at totality and permanence, at validity and meaning. And this points him beyond what is fragmentary and limited towards the transcendent. Seen in this way, aiming at transcendence is characteristic of every consciously worked out morality, even one that regards itself as merely human or non-religious. In our context it is perhaps important to see that we do not simply possess this fundamental orientation but must develop it. Christian faith offers itself as just such a fundamental orientation, and the decision of faith is the free act of fundamental orientation in response to the offer of Jesus Christ. This is an autonomous act of self-determination, albeit empowered and indebted. The existential 'Yes' to Jesus Christ (to his proclamation of God, to his perspectives of humanity, to his proclamation of the kingdom or reign of God as the realisation of definitive and ultimate justice) means decisively establishing oneself on the fundamental perspectives of his ethos. In this sense faith includes deciding in favour of a definite morality, given the possibility of choosing between several concepts of morality. This morality in the context of Christian faith is as a result not an élitist and particular one, and it cannot avoid the responsibility for a clear rational justification of actual ethical norms. It is a morality founded on reason because faith, precisely as an existential response to Jesus's challenge, is something based on and responding to the real situation of humanity.

Notes

1. For a brief indication see A. Auer 'Ein Modell theologisch-ethischer Argumentation: "Autonome Moral" ' in *Moralerziehung im Religionsunterricht* ed. A. Auer and others (Freiburg and elsewhere 1975) pp. 27–55.

2. See W. Korff *Theologische Ethik. Eine Einführung* (Freiburg 1975).

3. See D. Mieth *Moral und Erfahrung. Beiträge zur theologisch-ethischen Hermeneutik* (Fribourg, Switzerland and elsewhere 1977).

PART II

The Christian Ethic: An Ethic of Liberation?

Francisco Moreno Rejón

Seeking the Kingdom and its Justice: the Development of the Ethic of Liberation

THE MOST complete and representative work of theology of liberation shows beyond doubt that it contains ethical postulates, together with christological, biblical and ecclesiological ones.[1] Far from detracting from the validity of its approach, I would say that this is an indication of the radical novelty of this 'way of doing theology'. It seems logical that it should, at the outset, have emphasised the necessary unity and inter-connection between the various theological disciplines. This is the same approach proposed by Thomas Aquinas in the *Summa* when he states that Sacred Doctrine is one sole science (1a., q.1, a.3). This means that the theology of liberation can hardly be accused of usurpation, confusion or reductionism in the sphere of ethics.

But while any theological-moral approach cannot separate the boundaries between theology and morality with any precision in basic questions, there is an additional difficulty in the theology and ethic of liberation. This can be summed up by saying that the theology of liberation is the most 'moral' of theologies: firstly, because its methodology postulates praxis as the starting-point and goal of all theological reflection; secondly, because it requires every theologian, and so every moralist, as a Christian, to be committed, militant, as a *sine qua non* condition of undertaking moral theology.

The aim of this article is to offer some reflections on the development of the ethic of liberation and its historical and social context. I propose to divide it into three parts: first, a summary of the main contributions made to ethics by the theology of liberation; second, the historical-social, ecclesial and theological context in which the ethic of liberation has arisen and developed; third, the main themes and achievements of the ethic of liberation.

1. CONTRIBUTIONS MADE BY THE THEOLOGY OF LIBERATION TO ETHICS

The theology of liberation defines itself as a new way of understanding and doing theology. So a morality of liberation will not be one that includes a study of the theme of 'liberation' among its preoccupations, but one based on particular methodological postulates. What are these? Those most germane to our subject would seem to be the following:

(a) The concept of theology as a 'second step'

When theology is understood as 'critical reflection on the praxis of liberation in the light of the Word of God',[2] the first place is occupied by the praxis of liberation. Reflection comes later. Praxis becomes the starting-point of all theology and so clearly of ethics. But this is not all: the process through which praxis, which in the end is a gift from God, is submitted to critical reflection in the light of the Bible, in its turn produces a new praxis. The goal of theology is a new praxis. This is the methodological postulate which produces the necessary link between theology and liberation, the transformation of the world. This is what is meant by saying that the theology of liberation pays more heed to *orthopraxis* than to *orthodoxy*, that theology cannot be relegated to the limbo of theoretical reflection and that every theological postulate must have an ethical component.

(b) Theology in a prophetic vein

From its historical antecedents (such as Bartolomé de las Casas) and its written formulations, the theology of liberation has always had a prophetic ring. This takes it once more into the field of morals, but now not only in relation to theology, but also to pastoral practice. Pastoral activity and theology, understood in a prophetic sense, both have an ethical dimension. The statement of a theological position cannot leave us indifferent; on the contrary, it must always provoke the question: 'So what must we do?' (Acts 2:36–8). This is how the ethic of liberation goes beyond the sterility of so many ethical theories that remain trapped in the naturalist fallacy. A prophetic theology challenges, not only in the intellectual sphere, but also in that of praxis. The response has to be an ethical one: a practice of liberation.

(c) The mediating role of social analysis

The theology of liberation took the data of the social sciences into its methodology from the start, as a basic contribution to its discourse. Despite those critics who accuse it of excessive dependence on social analysis and over-fondness for Marxist analysis, it must be said that in general the use it has made of both has not been ingenuous but properly critical.[3] In the field of morals, this integration of social analysis into theological thought has enabled an inter-disciplinary ethical approach to develop.

Nevertheless, there is no denying that the choice of particular social data, conclusions or theories presupposes implicit decisions. On what grounds are some postulates critically accepted and not others? I think the answer is to be found in two underlying criteria which both condition and complement one another. The first is epistemological in character: the critical validation of a particular theory depends on its own scientific coherence. The second could be called ethical, in the sense that sciences are called upon not only to yield up their reality, but also to provide elements that contribute to their transformation. So the so-called neutrality of the sciences is not accepted here, for fear of falling into what has been called 'the ideology of those without an ideology'.[4]

(d) The role of utopia

One of the chief innovations of the theology of liberation has been to place utopia as the mediating axis between theological affirmations or propositions and specific actions. In this way, it is not the task of theology to work out tactics or give specific guidelines for action in a particular situation. Now utopia, as something that has not yet been brought about, cannot be grasped entirely by scientific-experimental methods. It includes elements which belong to the realm of the 'mythic'[5]—aspirations, values, etc. In this sphere it is more what is intuited than what has been achieved, but it is just because of this that the historical project has the power to push and pull people on, moving whole peoples in their struggle to build a new world. Here we are back in a field where the boundaries dividing theological from moral aspects are not at all clear, and both need to be linked to criteria stemming from other, non-theological disciplines.

To sum up, one can say that the theology liberation has opened up a way for an ethic of liberation to develop by providing it with the methodology which allows a morality to be formulated in accordance with these four characteristics: that it is practical, prophetic, critical and utopian. This would seem to offer sufficient scope for a dialogue between an ethic elaborated in the light of liberation and the approaches worked out by other currents of thought, with a good prospect for mutual enrichment.

2. THE CONTEXT IN WHICH THE ETHIC OF LIBERATION AROSE

Although the theology or ethic of liberation are often spoken of with the added qualification 'Latin-American', as though they belonged exclusively to this region, I do not think this is a completely accurate assessment. In effect, at the academic level, the ethics most widely taught in Latin America is a reflection and repetition of European morals.[6] But with this *caveat*, it is a clear fact that the theological current of liberation germinated and matured in Latin America between the years 1965 and 1975. Briefly, one can say that this was because Latin America at that time offered the necessary historico-social and ecclesial conditions for this to happen.[7] Let us briefly look at this.

(a) The historico-social context

This can be summarised as a situation characterised by the oppression-liberation dialectic. There was a realisation that the under-development and poverty of Latin America had to be seen in terms of dependence: the causal link between riches and poverty was brought to light. This, clearly, had consequences for an ethic that claimed to supply criteria of conduct that would be effective in transforming the situation. All reflection, as the philosophy of liberation has clearly shown,[8] takes place in the setting of particular historico-social co-ordinates which have to be fully understood not only as conditionings, but also as ethico-methodological options. All this implies that the ethic of liberation is produced:

From the periphery of the world: that is, from those countries generally placed under the heading of Third World. Dominated, dependent countries, with no real capacity for taking their own decisions.
From the periphery of society, the marginalised, those who do not count.
From the periphery of the city: from the slums and shanty towns, and, further out, from the shacks where the agricultural dispossessed, the subproletariat and oppressed ethnic groups live.
From the majorities: because, in fact, the peripheries of the world, of society, of the cities, are where most of the human race live. This is a fact that cannot be passed over in any moral reflection that seeks authenticity. Still less in a world that holds democracy to be a value of the highest order.
From the victims of a world in structural conflict. This means that ethics cannot be done from outside, but by those who feel themselves to be implicated, forced to take up options and take part in the process of liberation, which necessarily involves conflict.
From the underside of history: an expression coined by Gustavo Gutiérrez which sums up all the above and means taking on the viewpoint of the poor.[9]

(b) The ecclesial context

An oppressed continent taking stock of its oppression and setting itself firmly on the road to its liberation and, on the other hand, the presence of a believing people and ever more numerous Christian communities discovering in their faith the need to take an active part in the struggle for their liberation: these are the two circumstances which conjointly make Latin America the appropriate place for theology of liberation to germinate and develop in. They become the reference point for posing various ethical questions: love and the class struggle, violence, the 'situation of sin', etc. . .

In this ecclesial context the role of theologian and moralist cannot be reduced to that of a mere observer or interpreter of reality. Forming part of the people and of a Christian community, his moral reflection becomes the task of an 'organic intellectual . . . tied to the popular project of liberation'.[10]

(c) The theological context

Liberation theology and ethics grew from a markedly non-academic context. The attitudes and thoughts of Christians committed to their people are what make up the true ethic of liberation. Only occasionally and in a small proportion does this ethic born of experience and thought see the light of day as formulated morality.

There is another factor that conditions written production and explains the often fragmentary, occasional and provisional way it is presented. This is the precarious material conditions under which theological work has to be undertaken. First, there is a lack of people and time available: no one, in practice, can devote all his time to study and reflection. This is but one of the many tasks that a theologian or moralist finds he has to undertake. Second, there is a lack of adequate means and technical provision: in this sense, saying that the ethic of liberation is one that comes from the poor has to be taken literally, which involves suffering, with the poor, their lack of necessary means (even if, in this case, the 'necessary means' might be a good library). But at least there is always a Bible handy, and it might be worth noting at this point the privileged place which the Bible holds in the ethic of liberation and its christological and trinitarian character.[11]

3. THE DEVELOPMENT OF THE ETHIC OF LIBERATION

I said at the outset that the Latin-American theology of liberation has explicitly moral connotations. Yet some critics, such as M. Vidal, have attacked it for its 'ethical penury' or 'lack of an ethical theme'.[12] We need to be clear about what such phrases mean: the 'penury' here does not refer to the morality of everyday life, nor to lack of concern with ethical questions and problems. The lack is the absence of published studies giving a comprehensive account of themes of fundamental moral theology.[13] This is the tack that the ethic of liberation has set itself: to formulate the moral options, attitudes and values that shape the practice of Christians committed to the process of liberation in Latin America in a systematic fashion.

But we should not lose sight of the advances made in this field by the ethical philosophy of liberation, as evidenced particularly by the extensive and original works of Enrique Dussel, which have been widely influential. In this respect, the most significant development has been the transition in Latin-American philosophy, as shown in the works of Zubiri, from ontology to metaphysics.[14] This has produced a critical response to the ethic of the modern age as based on autonomy and typified as an ethic. It is seen as being: *progressivist* rather than new; *élitist* in the type of questions it tackles; *idealist*, in that it points to goals but ignores the means of reaching them; *privatising*: not so much individualist now, but personalist, arguing about concepts such as dialogue-encounter, but not those like domination-dependence; *functionalist*: its interlocutor is the modern-bourgeois world, which it legitimises, not the world of the poor and the people, whereas an ethic centred on liberation has to start with this basic question: How can we be good while liberating ourselves? The imperative resides not only in the 'being good', but equally in the 'liberating ourselves'. Morality has to make it a central function of its quest to contribute to solving the overall problem of Latin America: the situation of poverty, spoliation, oppression and death suffered by the vast majority of its believing and exploited people. Liberation thus becomes a basic ethical requirement.[15]

The theme of sin is indissolubly linked to that of liberation, and equally has to be referred to the three basic levels or dimensions: economic-socio-political, utopic-historical and redemptive-salvific.[16] In the one main ethical endeavour, liberation from all sin becomes the first concern of charity, not only in morals but in all theological endeavour. The old dichotomy between faith and works is superseded here, because the works of faith, expressed in love for the poor, are what finally save.

This brings us to the nucleus of the Gospel and of Christian ethics. Besides the well-known text in Matthew 25:31-46, we also need to note Paul's insistence that faith without love 'goes for nothing' (1 Cor. 13:2) and on 'faith that works through love' (Gal. 5:6).

4. FINAL CONSIDERATIONS

I should like to conclude by trying to set out in three short paragraphs the aspects that need to be borne in mind if the fruitful dialogue that needs to be undertaken between the ethic of liberation and the ethic of autonomy is to come about:

(a) Morality from oppression on the way to liberation

An authentic ethic faces the moralist with the need for his commitment to and insertion in the practice of liberation, and requires that his reflections possess the essential viability for them to have the historical efficacy they need. Moral theology must be tied to the Christian communities and to the popular movement as their basic and necessary mediation.

(b) Morality in the service of the people

The people here are to be understood in the sense of the poor, and so morality must be one that serves the interests of the poor people. To the extent that all ethics have a social function, contributing to the formation of an ethic of liberation is, as it were, forging a tool needed to advance the project of liberation. This is the meaning we give to the statement that morality must seek first the Kingdom and its justice (Matt. 6:33).

(c) Morality as spirituality and as science

Doing theology inescapably requires a spiritual experience. This needs not just good intentions or an original idea, but a determined effort to articulate the various sciences and tasks with the maximum critical rigour. Morality above all is the place where the theoretical and practical dimensions meet. A 'civil ethic' has been proposed recently[17] on the basis of the postulates of the morality of autonomy, and the characteristics of this 'civil ethic' would be: non-ideological, secular, democratic, non-confessional, pluralist. Such an ethic, it is claimed, would serve to harmonise interests and achieve progress in society. Such characteristics are well suited to the context of the developed democracies with their

D

bourgeois society and high degree of economic and political stability. They need an ethic to justify themselves: How is one to be good in such a society?

The ethic of liberation, on the other hand, stems from a torn and conflictive society, and therefore has to opt for one of the sides in the conflict. That means that, without being fanatical, it has to give priority to the quest for the poor. We are seeking an ethic that liberates, in which our neighbour and the Kingdom are the points of reference.

Translated by Paul Burns

Notes

1. G. Gutiérrez *A Theology of Liberation* (New York 1973; London 1974).

2. *Idem* p. 13.

3. See the excellent detailed study by M. Manzanera *Teología y salvación-liberación en la obra de Gustavo Gutiérrez* (Bilbao 1978) pp. 209–258.

4. C. Boff 'The Social Teaching of the Church and the Theology of Liberation: Opposing Social Practices?' in *Concilium* 150 (1981), at p. 17.

5. The word 'mythic' is here used in the sense given it by the Peruvian philosopher J. C. Mariategui in *El hombre y el mito: El alma matinal y otras estaciones del hombre de hoy* (Lima,[3] 1964).

6. As agreed by C. J. Snoek 'La teología moral en Brasil de hoy' in *Moralia* 4 (1982) pp. 67–81. What he says about Brazil is generally valid for the state of moral theology in the whole of Latin America.

7. I am here following the general argument of S. Silva Gotay in *El pensamiento cristiano revolucionario en América Latina y el Caribe* (Salamanca 1980).

8. See G. Marquínez Argote *Metafísica desde Latinoamérica* (Bogotá 1980) p. 8: 'The philosophy of liberation, then, is a way of thinking *in the situation* about our situation of dependence or oppression'. See also I. Ellacuria *Hacia una fundamentación filosófica del método teológico latinoaméricano: Liberación y cautiverio* (Mexico 1976) p. 626.

9. G. Gutiérrez *Desde el reverso de la historia* (Lima 1977). The same viewpoint can be found in O. Maduro 'Apuntes epistemológico-políticos para una historia de la teología en América Latina' in CEHILA *Materiales para una historia de la teología en América Latina* (San José 1981) pp. 19–38.

10. Gutiérrez, the work cited in note 1, at p. 58.

11. For the last three years a course has been held at the Bartolomé de las Casas Centre in Lima on 'Militant reading of the Bible'. The photocopied notes and accounts, from various sources, can be consulted at the Centre. This and other points are further developed in my 'Perspectivas para una ética de la liberación' in *Moralia* 4 (1982) pp. 135–150. J. Sobrino in his *Cristología desde América Latina (esbozo)* (Mexico 1977) p. xviii, states: 'the approach to the hermeneutical circle in the theology of liberation is trinitarian'. On the role of Jesus, his teaching and practice, in the popular morality of Latin-American communities, see the posthumous work by H. Echegarray *La práctica de Jesús* (Lima 1980).

12. M. Vidal *Moral de actitudes* III (Madrid 1979) pp. 127–129; G. Giménez *De la 'Doctrina social de la Iglesia' a la ética de liberación: Panorama de la teología latinoaméricana* II (Salamanca 1975) p. 46, speaks of the 'illegitimate usurpation' by the theology of liberation of the 'proper functions' of an ethic of liberation.

13. It is precisely the theologians and moralists of Latin America who have insisted on the need to approach ethical questions with care and depth: see R. Oliveros *Liberación y teología* (Lima 1980) p. 478; M. Manzanera the work cited in note 2, A. Moser 'Novas inquietaçoes na Teología Moral' in *Rev. Ecl. Bras.* 40 (1980) 5–61.

14. See E. Dussel *Método para una filosofia de la liberación: superación analéctica de la dialéctica hegeliana* (Salamanca 1974) p. 15: he opposes the ontology of totality by a metaphysic of otherness. G. Marquínez, in the work cited in note 8, at p. 105, proposes a 'definitive and unambiguous break with ontology'.

15. E. Dussel, in 'One Ethic and Many Moralities?', in *Concilium* 150 (1981), at p. 54, concludes that there is one absolute moral imperative: 'free the poor and the oppressed!'.

16. On this point, basic to theology, compare Gutiérrez *A Theology of Liberation*, ch. 3, with *Puebla*, paras. 322–326 and 483.

17. See M. Vidal 'La ética civil, riqueza del cuerpo social y justificación de la convivencia pluralista y democrática' in *Moralia* 5 (1983) 89–113.

Antonio Moser

The Representation of God in the Ethic of Liberation

AN ETHIC is not structured on its own basis, but depends directly on an anthropological concept, as well as on a theological one. In the broad sense, this theological concept also points to a Christology and an ecclesiology, while in the narrow sense it points to God. This is the sense I want to consider here.

Seeking this basic anthropological and theological framework points up an important challenge that must be faced in the much-discussed crisis of ethics. The practical and theoretical crisis, which has been in existence for several decades now, can well hide its existence among the shadows of badly assimilated concepts. Yet until we bring out into the light of day what kind of God and what kind of man we are talking about, there is no way of emerging from the shades of the crisis that hangs over the whole ethical scene.

The present crisis of ethics can be seen to reside in the fact that there are three models living together at the same time, not always in peace: the traditional model, the 'renewed' model, and the liberation model. I do not propose to dwell on the traditional model, since I hold it to be out of date, at least in theory, even though its practical influence cannot be discounted. I would rather consider the opposition between the renewed model, which sprang from the climate generated by Vatican II, and the liberation model, still emergent, which springs from the context of theology that has grown up in Latin America.

While the renewed model deals with concepts such as autonomy, heteronomy and theonomy, the liberation model seeks its theological basis in the exact extent to which it is conscious of being based on different anthropological and theological concepts, different because born of a different reality. So the question is to identify the God and man presupposed in the renewed model and the God and man presupposed in the ethic of liberation.

1. THE ANTHROPOLOGICAL CONCEPT OF THE RENEWED MODEL

One of the marks of the theology of the Council was its swing towards anthropocentrism. Conciliar theology took cognisance of the fact that theology is always a channel for an anthropological concept. Therefore, when it speaks of God, it speaks of man at the same time. And when it speaks of man, it speaks at the same time of God.

In ethical terms, this assimilation of the social sciences constituted a real revolution.

Renewed ethics no longer envisages a sort of superman, fearlessly facing up to the challenges of life. The heroes of old, sailing unhurt through life's storms through sheer force of character, are no more. Now we have simple mortals, bearing on their shoulders a greater or lesser burden of conditioning, determined to a greater or lesser degree, but always present and acting. This consciousness of the forces that condition human behaviour lies at the root of the release from the rigidity found in the traditional model.

Nevertheless, this anthropological swing, with all its benefits, still has its weak points. In ethical terms, it gave more weight to psychological factors than to social ones. There was no chance that it could have done otherwise. The man envisaged by the renewed model is a man divided, anguished, but at the same time privileged. Privileged, that is, from the social, economic and cultural standpoints. He may feel insecure in the depths of his being, but he is strengthened by the guarantees offered by his social context: employment, social security, good food, good living conditions, good housing, a good prospect of a tranquil old age, good medical services, an inalienable cultural heritage. Above all he draws strength from his achievements in a wide variety of scientific and technical fields. There may be various reasons why the man presupposed in the renewed model can lose his humanity, but his living conditions are not one of them.

The man in the renewed model is typified by success. The reverses he can suffer are but little waves ruffling his sea of tranquillity. So his ethical preoccupations are bound to be those of a liberal society and a culture of abundance. He seeks reasons to justify a greater degree of liberalism in ethical terms, and the result of this is, in fact, to confirm the *status quo*.

2. THE ANTHROPOLOGICAL CONCEPT OF THE ETHIC OF LIBERATION

The ethic of liberation is still at an embryonic stage, being the least developed sector of the theology of liberation. Like the theology, it did not spring from any air-conditioned study, but from the suffocating heat of the practice of a Church set not in the world of progress, but in the sub-world made up the great mass of people who are deprived of the most basic elements of human existence.

Understanding the reality of this sub-world is the first great challenge facing an ethic of liberation. This means avoiding at all costs the pitfalls attendant on an ingenuous or functionalist approach, both marked by the dominant ideology. What is needed is a critical-radical understanding, one that breaks with the determinisms of the system, digging deeper among the roots of the brutal reality with which it is confronted. Only this type of investigation, calling the whole socio-economic system into question, will be capable of helping ethics go beyond the limits imposed by indignation or 'assistanceism' and emerge within a liberating practice, at the service of a new reality.

The man envisaged by the ethic of liberation is a man marked by suffering, suffering caused by deep poverty, widespread and deliberate. The features this ethic looks at are not the well-rounded faces of those who have been well nourished and cared for: they are 'the features of children ground down by poverty before being born . . .; of young people adrift because they can find no place in society . . .; of natives . . .; of Afro-Americans, living in sub-human ghettoes, who can be considered the poorest of the poor . . .; of peasants . . . deprived of land . . .; of underpaid workers . . . of the under-employed or the unemployed . . .; of the marginalised . . .; of the ever-increasing number of old people . . .'[1]

The starting-point for an ethic of liberation cannot, therefore, be either man in the abstract or man marked by success. Its starting-point has to be man mutilated, oppressed by a situation of screaming injustice. And its objective has to be above all to generate a practice of liberation, capable of dragging this man free of the evils of oppression and bringing him more favourable conditions of life.

3. THE GOD WE MAKE

The theological context in which the renewed model was developed has two complementary facets: secularisation and atheism. From the angle of secularisation, its point of reference is that of the majority of mankind. Modern man, drunk with his successes, cannot be convinced either by a God who makes up for his deficiencies or by one who calls his triumphs into question. This is why 'the death of God' is the fullest expression of the deep changes brought about in man himself. The abandonment of a theological language indicates first and foremost the abandonment of a cultural tradition based wholly on the sacred. 'When we speak of the death of God, . . . we cannot escape the emergence of images that indicate the collapse of a cultural tradition: the universe loses its centre, a funeral cortège is drawn across cosmic and metaphysical spaces, once charged with meaning, now cold, empty and silent, with the sun set on them for ever. This is the silent requiem which the heavenly hosts intone before the death of life itself.'[2]

The characteristic of secularised man is no longer to ask certain questions about God. This does not mean that the problems faced by such questions have gone away. It simply means that certain questions have been forbidden or repressed. 'We live in an age which forbids mystery—which it relegates to the "primitives", ignorant and suffering . . . The great dogma of the world that calls itself scientific is that reality is self-explanatory and that reason disposes of the instruments necessary to decipher the enigma it is faced with.'[3] The religious world seems to belong to a past age and God to be a being who may exist but has been eclipsed.

In such a climate, atheism appears not only a possible, but a fully reasonable hypothesis. There is no doubt that atheism seems a great challenge to renewed theology, and so a great occasion for the purification of theology and religion. Atheism is not brought about by itself; it is the effect of the dislocation of human experience from religious categories. So contemporary atheism becomes a clear indication of the gap opened up by time between institutionalised religions and people of our age. These religions tend to put forward an image of God that has stopped in time. And a God who has stopped in time can only be an idol, since the true God is the one who does not allow himself to be caught up in the schemes of men of any given time. He must always be the God who was, is and will be. God becomes a sort of sphinx, who never gives up his deepest secret and never shows his true face. If his secret were discovered, he would fade away. He lives off his secret. And so every traveller who passes his forehead will see him and describe him as something different, since the sphinx is in some way a projection of everyman. If God made us in his image and likeness, then we too make him in our image and likeness.

Atheism keeps religions in the provisionality of a never-finished quest. In this sense contemporary atheism is essential to the theism of religions: it forces them to discern the passage of time, which is full of new signs of God, who never reveals himself completely to men, never completely uncovers his face, but shows himself in day-to-day events.

This background explains why the ethic of the renewed model is determined to find a basis outside a presupposition of the existence of God. A secular ethic is a necessity for a world in which atheism seems a real alternative, and in which God can never be captured in one's sights.

4. GOD THE LIBERATOR

Of course the problem of God is present in the theology of liberation. Nevertheless, it is not as fully worked out as in European theology. This, which can at first sight seem a deficiency, is in fact the result of a different understanding of the problem of God, which stems from a different understanding of reality. What is sought is not to uncover the true essence of God, but to experience the reality of God in the bringing-about of his

Kingdom.[4] The pressure of social problems leads to greater emphasis being placed on Christology and ecclesiology, which bear more directly on liberating praxis.

This does not mean, though, that there is no concept of God present in the theology of liberation. It is presupposed, hardly made explicit, and above all oriented in a different direction. The great question that has to be raised is not why so many people either deny or affirm God, but what the particular individual who accepts or rejects God is doing and seeking. What is God's effect on the specific existence of the persons who make up a society?[5] The strictly theological problem consists in rediscovering the living God in the face of other divinities who lead to death in the name of God. In other words, the confrontation is not between God and atheism, but between faith and idolatry. This is why the representation of God underlying the ethic of liberation is that of the God of Life, who makes himself known in human history, taking the side of the poor and seeking to set up his Kingdom for them.

(a) The God of life

The struggle in which we are engaged in Latin America is above all a struggle for survival. Beset by economic, social, political and cultural aggressions, the masses of this continent see death surrounding them on all sides. While an élite enjoys the privileges typical of a world of abundance, the great majority are continually faced with the virtual impossibility of surviving. Millions of poor Lazaruses batter ineffectually at the door of the rich merchant.

From the depths of the poverty in which they are submerged, the poor masses can expect nothing from the ruling classes and their idols, represented by wealth unjustly accumulated, by the vast estates resulting from expropriation, and by the National Security forces which terrorise them.

It is in this context that the peoples of Latin America, justly characterised as poor and believing, can find only one way out: to call on Him who gave them life. Popular religiosity, with its unbreakable sense of the sacred and the divine, is the force that sustains them on their way. This context is the background against which the defence and promotion of life itself become theological problems of the first order. The only theological counterpoint to the idols of death is the God of life.

(b) God becomes present in history

The representation of God put forward by the theology of liberation is that of the God of the Bible, not the God of the philosophers. Born of its vital contact with the Ecclesial Base Communities, this theology can only feed itself from the same source that feeds these communities. There the Word of God is read and commented on not as history of past events, but as the story of the present. It is in the conflict between the Word of God and actual reality that the Base Communities seek light and strength for their journey. And it is from the same conflict that the theology of liberation draws its prophetic power. This is why its picture of God cannot be one of a distant and indifferent God, but only of a present, active God.

In contrast to the idols, who 'have mouths, but never speak, eyes, but never see, ears, but never hear, noses, but never smell, hands, but never touch, feet, but never walk' (Ps. 115:5–7), the God of the Bible is a God who sees the sufferings of his people, hears their cries, challenges the powerful, intervenes in human history, acting always in favour of the oppressed. The definition that Jesus gives of his mission, in his first speech (Luke 4:18–19) confirms and clarifies God's actions in human history. He comes, in the name of God, to 'bring the good news to the poor, to proclaim liberty to captives ... to set the downtrodden free' and so to usher in a new reality in the world of mankind.

(c) God takes the part of the poor

The 'preferential option' for the poor, officially adopted at Medellín and Puebla, has become a general order setting the direction of the Church in Latin America. This option, clearly, has not pleased everyone. It is rejected by the military regimes and even by some conservative members of the hierarchy. The very expression causes shudders in all those interested in maintaining the *status quo* in society. On the other hand it has been enthusiastically welcomed by all those engaged in the struggle for social justice. The preferential option for the poor has become a sort of touchstone by which individuals and groups can be measured.

Yet there is nothing fortuitous or even gratuitous about the expression: it expresses the conscience of a Church that sees its emergence from a so-called neutral stance as a question of fidelity to the Gospel. There is a strictly theological understanding underlying the preferential option for the poor: that the God of revelation is not a God who intervenes in a neutral fashion in human affairs. He is a God who takes the part of the weak, the poor and the oppressed.

God's option showed itself in his choice of a people who were to build a history based on law, justice and brotherhood (Isa. 58:2ff): a weak people of no importance in the context of their age (Deut. 26:4ff). The same option is prolonged throughout the history of Israel, which is continually shown that God has his favourites. He is the Lord who guarantees the rights of the poor (Exod. 22:21–22); who 'sees justice done for the orphan and the widow' (Deut. 10:18); 'gives justice to those denied it, gives food to the hungry, gives liberty to prisoners. Yahweh restores sight to the blind, Yahweh straightens the bent . . .' (Ps. 146:5–7).

The same option can be seen in the Chosen One of God, who 'will free the poor man who calls on him, and those who need help, he will have pity on the poor and feeble, and save the lives of those in need' (Ps. 72:12–13). Beginning with his discourse in the synagogue at Nazareth, Jesus makes quite clear that the fulfilment of his mission is intimately linked to transforming action in favour of the marginalised of every sort. From this point on the difficult thing is not to see that the poor are God's favourites;[6] the difficult thing is failing to see that any reading of the Gospel that excludes the poor from the place of honour is a reading based on an ideological preconception.

CONCLUSION

To construct a system of ethics theologically on the basis of putting the poor and their liberation in the first place can seem a daring thing to do. Which in fact it is. Throughout the history of ethics, it has always thought *of* the poor, but never *from* them; it has thought of the poor from the point of view of the rich, thinking that touching the hearts of the rich is going to benefit the poor. The ethic of liberation, founded on a different anthropological and theological understanding, seeks to turn the process upside-down: to think from the poor, with them and in favour of them. This represents a greater revolution by far than that brought about by Vatican II.

The renewed model broadened the horizon of ethics, but did not shift its centre of interest. The liberation model tries precisely to shift the centre of interest. This leads it in the first place to reverse the order of importance of human problems. In the first rank it sets problems related to life, death, injustice, poverty, hunger, sickness, ignorance, land, participation, etc. Not only is the order of importance inverted, but the way of approaching problems is also fundamentally different. Those who enjoy good living conditions will have one outlook on life; those who have continually to face up to conditions of death will have another; those who are able to procure good health care will see things from one point of view; those who lack even the most basic sanitation will see them from another.

Furthermore, the objective of the renewed model lies within the system, or within a reformed version of it. The objective of the liberation model is primarily social and 'revolutionary'. What it aims at are not long-term improvements, but a new whole embracing the socio-economic, political, cultural and even religious complex.

There is nothing arbitrary about such a shift. It springs from one way of looking at God and man. While the renewed model responds to the needs of the well-off minority, the liberation model responds to the needs of the absolute majority of the human race who are at present deprived of their rights. While the renewed model stems from an outdated representation of God, the liberation model stems from the representation that the impoverished, inspired by the Word of God, make of God: the One who 'hears the cry of the oppressed' (Josh. 24:38), and comes to set his people free. This is why the ethic of liberation shows a prophetic daring that confounds the powerful of this world. It is the expression of the wisdom revealed to little ones (Matt. 11:25–26) who are on the way to doing the will of the Father. The crisis affecting ethics will not be resolved by means of new theories, but only by ethics placing itself in the service of the cause of the Kingdom, and not of those who rule.

Translated by Paul Burns

Notes

1. *Puebla* (Washington & Slough, 1979) nn. 32–39.
2. R. Alves *O Enigma da Religião* (Petropolis[2] 1979) p. 31.
3. Alves, the work cited in note 2, at p. 33.
4. See J. Sobrino *Resurrección de la verdadera Iglesia* (Santander 1981) p. 45.
5. See J.-L. Segundo *A nossa idéia de Deus* (São Paulo 1977) p. 17.
6. *Puebla* n. 1143.

Tony Misfud

The Development of a Liberation Ethic in the Documents of the Church since Vatican II

IN THE general audience he gave on Wednesday 21st February 1979, John Paul II said: 'Liberation is certainly a reality of faith, one of the fundamental biblical themes, profoundly present in Christ's saving mission, the work of redemption, in his teaching. This theme has never ceased to constitute the content of the spiritual life of Christians. The Conference of Latin American bishops testifies that this theme is returning in a new historical context; this is why it must be taken up again in the Church's teaching, in theology and pastoral work. It must be taken at its full depth and Gospel authenticity.'

1. A CHURCH INVOLVED WITH HISTORY

The Second Vatican Council marked a new stage in the history of the Church. The bishops from all over the world echoed the 'joys and hopes, the griefs and the anxieties of the men of this age, especially those who are poor or in any way afflicted' because they felt themselves 'truly and intimately linked with mankind and its history' (*Gaudium et Spes*, 1: *Documents of Vatican II*, ed. Walter M. Abbot, p. 199). The missionary spirit of the people of God was expressed in terms of an involvement with the human race in its actual situation in history in an attempt to collaborate in the achievement of 'that brotherhood of all men' to carry forward the work of Christ himself (*ibid.*, 3: Abbot, *op. cit.*, p. 201).

This is a Church which is open to the demands of history and shares the task of a humanity called to 'establish a political, social and economic order which will to an even better extent serve man and help individuals as well as groups to affirm and develop the dignity proper to them' (*ibid.*, 9: Abbot, *op. cit.*, p. 206).

The ecclesiological view of the Council commits the people of God to a responsibility for human history, discerning the signs of the times. 'Men are not deterred by the Christian message from building up the world, or impelled to neglect the welfare of their fellows. They are rather, more stringently bound to do these very things.' (*ibid.*, 34: Abbot, *op. cit.*, p. 233). The position of the Council has been reaffirmed by later documents. But can we speak of a Christian involvement in terms of a liberation ethic formulated in the documents of the Church?

2. AN 'OFFICIAL' LIBERATION ETHIC?

The reply to the question can take two methodological forms: (*a*) offer a reply from the standpoint of a previously formulated liberation ethic, or (*b*) seek in the texts themselves for certain characteristic remarks on the concept of 'liberation' which add up to a liberation ethic. It is not easy to choose the right course, but I think the second is the more likely one, especially because as far as I know, there exists no definition of a liberation ethic. Moreover, this way avoids the danger of manipulating a selection of texts to support a particular thesis.

In recent years the theme of liberation has been present in the official teaching of the Church. We will take as reference documents: *Populorum Progressio* (1967), the World Synod of Bishops on Justice (1971), *Octogesima Adveniens* (1971) *Evangelii Nuntiandi* (1975) and *Laborem Exercens* (1981), (hereafter referred to as *P.P.*, *Synod*, *O.A.*, *E.N.*, *L.E.* respectively). These documents are examples of universal teaching. The documents of Medellín *The Church in the present transformation of Latin America in the light of the Council* (1968), and of Puebla (1979) give the teaching of the pastoral *magisterium* of Latin America. This is relevant because Latin America has produced the most vigorous theological reflection on the theme of liberation.

3. THE ETHICAL SIGNIFICANCE OF THE CONCEPT OF 'LIBERATION'

The concept of 'liberation' is nothing new in the official teaching of the Church. From the above-mentioned documents, I propose six central statements which reveal the meaning and ethical richness of the word 'liberation'.

(*a*) The historical context itself highlights the theological relevance of the concept of liberation

This is not a theological 'fashion' but a theological 'necessity' in the face of an oppressive reality which denies the saving presence of God. It is the *context* of an unjust reality which requires a reading of the Gospel in terms of liberation. 'Listening to the cry of those who suffer violence and are oppressed by unjust systems and structures, and hearing the appeaal of a world that by its perversity contradicts the plan of its Creator, we have shared our awareness of the Church's vocation to be present in the heart of the world by proclaiming the Good News to the poor, freedom to the oppressed, and joy to the afflicted.' (*Synod*, 5 (*Vatican Collection* II ed. Austin Flannery OP, pp. 695–696. See *Puebla*, 487). The Church feels called to denounce injustice and even more it feels 'the duty of helping this liberation, of bearing witness on its behalf and of assuring its full development.' (*E.N.*, 30: Flannery *op. cit.*, p. 724).

(*b*) Faith in God Defender of the poor and oppressed leads us to proclaim a Liberating God

'In the Old Testament God reveals himself to us as the liberator of the oppressed and the defender of the poor, demanding from man faith in him and justice towards man's neighbour. It is only in the observance of the duties of justice that God is truly recognised as the liberator of the oppressed.' (*Synod* 32: Flannery, *op. cit.*, p. 701. See *ibid.*, 6; *Medellín*, Introduction, 6; *Puebla*, 1142.)

(*c*) The work of Jesus is to be seen as liberating action

'Christ lived his life in the world as a total giving of himself to God for the salvation and liberation of men. In his preaching he proclaimed the fatherhood of God towards all men and the intervention of God's justice on behalf of the needy and the oppressed.' (*Synod*, 33: Flannery *op. cit.*, p. 701. See *Medellín*, Justice, 3; *Puebla*, 1145.)

(d) Preaching the Gospel implies liberation from all oppression.

The Church's mission is to preach the Gospel, that is 'the carrying forth of the Good News to every sector of the human race so that by its strength it may enter into the hearts of men and renew the human race', converting 'both the individual consciences of men and their collective conscience, all the activities in which they are engaged and, finally, their lives and the whole environment which surrounds them.' (*E.N.*, 18: Flannery, *op. cit.*, pp. 718–9). Preaching the Gospel means bringing a message of freedom from all oppression (*Ibid.*, 9 and 29; cf. *Puebla*, 480).

(e) Liberation is a historical mediation of the good news

'The mission of preaching the Gospel dictates at the present time that we should dedicate ourselves to the liberation of man even in his present existence in this world. For unless the Christian message of love and justice shows its effectiveness through action in the cause of justice in the world, it will only with difficulty gain credibility with the men of our times.' (*Synod*, 37: Flannery, *op. cit.*, p. 702. See *Medellín*, Justice, 4; *E.N.*, 9 and 31; *Puebla* 483 and 490.) This does not mean a superficial verbal liberation; it involves the denunciation and overcoming of the cause of oppression (see *Puebla*, 1146).

(f) Christian liberation is an option for the poor against injustice

'We affirm the need for conversion of the whole Church to a preferential option for the poor, with regard to their total liberation' (*Puebla*, 1134), and this option means 'a constant conversion and purification in all Christians with the aim of identifying more fully day by day with the poor Christ and with the poor' (*Puebla*, 1140). This option is the criterion of our faithfulness in following Christ. 'Because the poor are the first for whom his mission and Gospel are intended, this is the pre-eminent sign and proof of Jesus' mission' (*Puebla*, 1142). John Paul II speaks of service of the exploited as an ecclesial mission of 'verification of its faithfulness to Christ, so that it can really be the "Church of the poor" ' (*L.E.*, 8).

The concept of 'liberation' is an ethical one in that it implies an *orthodoxy* (belief in God the Father of all men and in his Son Jesus who took up the cause of the poor in order to establish a genuine brotherhood) and also an *orthopraxis* (the Christian mission to denounce unjust structures that contradict God's liberating plan).

The ethical originality of the task of liberation is provided by the person of Jesus Christ. His liberating action is the force behind a radical involvement in the struggle against injustice which creates poverty and outrages against marginalised humanity, because the divine image in it is 'darkened and mocked' (*Puebla*, 1142). In the exploited of the earth we recognise the 'suffering features of Christ the Lord which question and challenge us' (*Puebla*, 31; cf. *Ibid.*, 32–39).

The official teaching of the Latin American Church makes an ethical demand which begins with a preferential option for the poor and seeks the historical bringing about of the whole liberation of the whole person and of all people without reduction (either of the 'spiritual' or the 'temporal' kind) or identification (the reduction of the Kingdom to a precise moment of history). This radical involvement, this solidarity with the poor and the oppressed, is a moral obligation (see *E.N.*, 29–36; *Puebla*, 480–490).

In this task of transforming history, the Christian is called not to resort to 'any kind of violence or the dialectic of the class struggle' (*Puebla*, 486; see *E.N.*, 37). Furthermore criteria are offered for the discernment of the difference between liberation and a non-evangelical ideology: at the level of *content* there is the requirement of faithfulness to the Word of God, the living Tradition of the Church and its *magisterium*. At the level of *attitudes* there is the requirement of a sense of communion with the bishops, in the first place, and with the other sectors of the people of God; making an effective contribution to the creation of community; acting with loving concern towards the needy; the effort to supply their needs, seeing in them the living image of Jesus (see *Puebla*, 489). It is very important to stress this strong emphasis on *orthopraxis* with an ecclesial and social way of life as a criterion for discernment. In other words the Christian mission can only be judged by its actions.

4. NOTES FOR AN ETHIC OF LIBERATION

Now that we have clarified the meaning of liberation in the official teaching of the Church, we can draw up an outline schema, of course rudimentary, of a liberation ethic. *Ethical indignation* produced by the presence of injust structures affecting thousands of victims every day challenges ethical reflection to urgent *critical-utopian* discourse with an *ethico-prophetic* methodology which takes as its starting point a *social concern* of *solidarity with the oppressed*, the living images of God crucified.

(*a*) The condition in which the great majority of humanity lives produces an *ethical indignation* because the most fundamental rights of the human person are not respected (food, lodging, political participation etc). Furthermore it is scandalous to see this wretched reality in those countries whose rulers call themselves Christians. This human tragedy denies the vocation of every human being as children of God and brothers and sisters of each other (see *Synod*, 3; *O.A.*, 2, 3, 10, 15–18; *Medellín*, Message 2 and 4; *ibid.*, Justice, 1 and 2; *Puebla*, 27–50, 55–62, 127–130, 487, 834–840). The starting point for ethical discussion is the intolerable situation of marginalised humanity; it must speak for those who are forsaken and condemned to silence. Ethics becomes the voice of the voiceless.

(*b*) This human tragedy forces ethics into a *critical-utopian* view of human history; not an apocalyptic stance of detachment from history but an utopian involvement in the building of the Kingdom (see *Medellín*, Catechesis, 4). It is important to overcome any dichotomy between what we believe and what we do. This means that we must 'end the separation between faith and life, because in Christ Jesus the only thing that counts is "faith that works through love" (Gal. 5:6)' (*Medellín*, Message, 6; see *E.N.*, 29; *Puebla*, Message, 3). The tragic situation of marginalised humanity requires the creation of a social conscience (*Medellín*, Justice, 17), the awakening of a critical sense (*Ibid.*, Peace, 25; *Synod*, 53), and a creative effort (*Medellín*, Message, 3) to undertake and carry out the task of transforming society. 'In this daily more determined will to transform the world we cannot fail to keep on discovering traces of God's image in man, as a potent dynamism' (*Medellín*, Introduction, 4; cf. *Ibid.*, 5). A critical-utopian view tries to find the root causes of marginalisation of man by man (*Synod*, 9–12; *O.A.*, 15; *Puebla*, 64–70 and 1254–1293). This position does not exempt the Church from serious self-criticism (see *Puebla*, 1135).

(*c*) A critical view of historical reality whose point of reference is the utopia of the Kingdom of God, requires an *ethico-prophetic* methodology. A critical reading of reality and a utopian discernment of human history leads to liberating action. The see-judge-act schema is valid if to criticism (seeing) and utopia (judging) we add action (cf. *Synod*, 2; *O.A.*, 4; Puebla, 1307). 'It is not enough to state principles, affirm intentions, underline crying injustices and utter prophetic denunciations; these words have no real weight, if they are not accompanied in each one of us by an increased awareness of our own responsibility and by effective action' (*O.A.*, 48). Furthermore, the historical situation 'requires clarity to see, lucidity to diagnose and solidarity to act' (*Medellín*, Message, 3); this means action in solidarity with the poor and marginalised. The methodology consists in *reading* with a preferential option, *judging* from God's viewpoint, from whom the poor are his 'best beloved' (see *Puebla*, 1143) and *acting* in solidarity with them.

(*d*) Ethics must feel a deep *social concern* for the marginalised. 'It is not just a question of overcoming hunger or of decreasing poverty. The struggle against destitution, although urgent and necessary, is not enough. We need to build a world in which every human being, without regard to race, religion or nationality, can live a fully human life, freed from the slaveries imposed on him by other human beings and an insufficiently mastered natural world; a world in which freedom is not an empty word and in which the poor Lazarus can sit down at the same table as the rich man' (*P.P.*, 47). The reality of the social dimension of sin (see *Synod*, 5, 31, 53, 60; *Puebla*, 70, 73, 185, 186, 281, 452, 515, 1032, 1269) requires a personal conversion translated into a struggle for the social transformation of sinful structures (see *Synod*, 16; *O.A.*, 45; *E.N.*, 18 and 36; *Puebla*, 358, 1134, 1155–1158). 'The originality of the Christian message does not consist directly in the affirmation of a need to change structures, but in its insistence on human conversion, which then requires this change in structures. We will not get a new continent without new and renewed structures; above all, there will be no new continent without new people, who know in the light of the Gospel how to be truly free and responsible' (*Medellín*, Justice, 3). Thus 'service of the poor is the most important, although not the only, way to follow Christ' (*Puebla*, 1145; see 1140–1147).

(*e*) Social concern becomes translated into an ethical duty of *solidarity with the oppressed*. The tragic and sinful reality, since 'everything that affects human dignity, wounds, in a certain manner, God himself' (*Puebla*, Message, 3) points us towards a solidarity *with* and a programme *against* (see *Puebla*, 1154). That is to say, solidarity with the oppressed implies a struggle against injustice in the name of God the Father. It is not just a solidarity for but a solidarity *with*, which stresses the role of the oppressed as protagonist in self organisation, defence and advancement so that they can join and share with equal right and dignity at the human table. 'Human advancement must be the aim of our action for the poor, so that we respect their personal dignity and teach them to help themselves' (*Medellín*, Poverty of the Church 11; see *ibid.*, Peace, 27 and Education, 8; *Puebla*, 135, 474, 1153, 1162, 1163, 1220; *O.A.*, 43; *Synod*, 17, 54, 73). In this way it is the people who become the Church's challenger, and not the State (cf. *Medellín* Youth, 15; *Ibid.*, Pastoral Care of Elites, 21; *Puebla*, 144), seeking the conversion of the oppressor (cf. *Puebla*, 1155, 1156). The Church in opting for the human being and human dignity denounces the two systems of capitalist liberalism and Marxist collectivism (see *Medellín*, Justice, 10; *Puebla*, 311–313, 542–546; *L.E.*, 13 and 14), realising that 'the fear of Marxism prevents many from facing the oppressive reality of liberal capitalism' (*Puebla*, 92); and also the State ideology of National Security (see *Puebla*, 314, 547–550) and the consumer mentality (see *Puebla*, 62, 311, 435, 496, 834). This is why we need to formulate the inalienable values of freedom and equality which allow a worthy participation in the political and economic process without marginalisation of social sectors who have no opportunity of exercising their right and their duty as citizens (see *Synod*, 3, 9, 18; *O.A.*, 22; *Medellín*, Justice, 7, 16; *Puebla*, 327 and 502). Peace cannot be built on the silence of the oppressed; 'the dialogue for peace is inseparable from the dialogue for justice' (John Paul II, Peace Day, 1st January 1983, 10).

The official teaching of the Church offers guidelines for the formulation of a liberation ethic against all that oppresses human beings in history today.

5. TOWARDS AN ETHIC OF LIBERATION

There have already been attempts to formulate an ethic of liberation.[1] I believe that an ethic of liberation must respect and include the following elements:

(*a*) a *Christian* ethic, with the person and action of Jesus Christ as the force inspiring the work of transformation at the personal and the social level;

(*b*) an ethic which allows itself to be challenged by *reality*, that is not just a question of translating faith into works, but reality itself is the starting point for a reading of the signs of the times and the ethical verification of our faith;

(*c*) an ethic *from the standpoint of marginalised humanity*, since the poor and oppressed are the most important 'ethical touchstone' by which we can read reality and understand the Good News;

(*d*) an ethic of *solidarity* proposing the crucial values of an alternative common project formulated from the viewpoint and taking up the cause of the poor, because only thus can we speak of a real option for the poor against poverty. Such solidarity does not mean a paralysing 'paternalism' but support for a popular protagonism in the sense that the oppressed and the marginalised are forces, like others, of history;

(*e*) an ethic of *discernment* capable of taking on the present conflict and directing it responsibly;

(*f*) an ethic of *wholeness*, seeking liberation in all human and social dimensions and a *universal* ethic calling upon us all to take up the cause of the poor and impoverished.

We invite all, without any distinction of class, to accept and take on the cause of the poor as if they were accepting and taking on their own cause, the cause of Christ himself. 'As you did it to one of the least of these my brothers, you did it to me (Matt. 25:40)' (*Puebla*, Message, 3).

Translated by Dinah Livingstone

Note

1. See the very interesting contributions by M. Vidal 'Teologia de la liberacion y etica social cristiana', *Studia Moralia* XV (1977) 207–218 and 'La preferencia por el pobre, criterio de moral', *Studia Moralia* XX/2 (1982) 277–304 (with a bibliography on the subject). *Hacia una moral liberadora; ensayo de una teologia moral fundamental desde America Latina* (Santiago, CIDE, 1982) is my own first attempt at a systemisation of fundamental morality from the point of view of liberation.

Enrique Dussel

An Ethics of Liberation: fundamental hypotheses

IF IT required an effort on the part of Paul Tillich to explain in the United States the different function of the Church in Europe, how much greater will be the effort required of a theologian from Latin America, from the peripheral world, to explain the critical function of ethics in situations in need of profound social change?[1]

1. MORALITIES INSIDE THE SYSTEMS

In the last 50 years there has taken place in the United States and Europe a shift from criticism of the system as a totality to merely reformist criticism of the social order. One significant date is 13th April 1931, when the name of Tillich[2] appeared on the list which Hitler's national-capitalist government had drawn up of intellectuals who were 'critical' of the system.[3] Tillich himself was to write later that 'the fact that National Socialism crushed the religious Socialist movement and drove it underground or into exile, as it did the many creative movements of the twenties, could not prevent the spread of these ideas in churches and cultures beyond the borders of Germany and Europe'.[4]

In 1932 Reinhold Niebuhr published his *Moral Man and Immoral Society*,[5] and Emil Brunner *The Divine Imperative*.[6]

The crisis of 1929—the crisis of capitalism and the growing repression of the working class of the 'centre'—the victory of the Russian revolution and the rise of Stalin produced an upheaval in theology. The 'early' Tillich, the 'early' Niebuhr (and a little earlier the 'early' Barth) talk to us about moving from a critique of the system to a prudent reformist morality, 'Christian realism': 'The illusion is dangerous because it encourages terrible fanaticism,' was the ending of Niebuhr's book,[7] and Tillich, who had written *The Socialist Decision*,[8] was subsequently to move much more towards a theology of culture. Another movement of great importance finally died in these years, the 'social gospel'[9] Richard Ely's *French and German Socialism* (New York 1883) or Washington Gladden's *Tools and the Man. Property and Industry under the Christian Law* remain impressive today, particularly Chapter 10 of Gladden's book, 'Christian Socialism',[10] where he explains, 'In the latest books on socialism we always find a chapter entitled "Christian Socialism". Has this phrase any meaning? Is Christianity in some sense socialist, or perhaps socialism is Christian?"[11] What is important today is not the explanations—nor even Gladden's criticisms of Marx (which are excellent, because he knew Marx);[12] what is important is the Christian attitude of criticism of the capitalist system as a whole. Walter Rauschenbusch forcefully criticised 'our semi-Christian social order', which he described as 'under the Law of Profit'.[13] These Christians, who were linked with the social struggles of the period from the end of the nineteenth century to 1929, were buried by the violence of European and North American capitalism between the two wars (1914–1945) for the leadership of that capitalism from which the United States emerged victorious (and the Commonwealth, like Germany and Japan, defeated).

The postwar moral theologies could not break out of the reformist mould. They accept the system as it is; they suggest *partial* reforms. This is the inescapable conclusion of an examination of the main moral treatises.[14]

It is interesting to consider Brunner's book of 1932. While it is far superior in its treatment to the Catholic treatises of the period, it manages first to criticise capitalism ('Capitalism is a form of economic anarchy; the Christian is therefore obliged to fight against it and for a true social order'),[15] but subsequently also criticises actual socialism.[16] In the same way Helmut Thielicke, in his *Theologische Ethik*,[17] clearly shows his reformism in the section on 'revolution as a last resort'.[18] As in the works previously mentioned, and in those to be mentioned later, there is of course no reference to the oppression of the peripheral countries, even though it has been clearly posed theologically as long ago as the sixteenth century by Bartolomé de las Casas.

We find a movement from criticism of capitalism to a critical acceptance of it, leading finally, in the present crisis, to a moral justification of it. The whole of the North American neo-conservative movement (and the European conservative movement)[19] could assent to the conclusions of Robert Benne, in his book *The Ethic of Democratic Capitalism. A Moral Reassessment.*[20] In his Chapter 7, 'The Virtues of Democratic Capitalism', he writes, 'Democratic capitalism has been an undervalued social system, especially by the liberal intellectual community, both religious and secular. We have attempted to challenge that underassessment by emphasising the values and achievements that are often overlooked.'[21]

For these moralities which remain within the system, radical criticism of the system is anarchy, fanaticism; it is the irrationality of 'historicism' apparently refuted by Popper, translated into economic terms by Milton Friedman in the neo-capitalism of the 'self-regulating equilibrium of the free market'. Within this framework moral theologies have to consider 'norms' (laws), values, virtues, good and evil, the problem of language, of technology, and even of peace, without ever questioning the 'system' as such. Analytic thought is fundamentally hostile to any dialectical proposition.

2. THE ETHICS OF LIBERATION

In contrast, for the Christians of the countries which are peripheral to capitalism and the oppressed classes of those countries, the irreversible crisis came after the second war for the leadership of capitalism. Ten years after the end of the war the expansion of North American capitalism destroyed the endeavours of peripheral national capitalism. (In 1954 Vargas committed suicide in Brazil, in 1955 Perón fell in Argentina, Rojas Pinilla fell in Colombia in 1957. Nasser in Egypt and Sukarno in Indonesia are parallel cases in Africa and Asia. In the countries of the periphery 'populism' was the last effort of a non-dependent, autonomous *national capital*, under the leadership of a national bourgeoisie, such as the Congress Party in India.) The crisis of the model of 'dependent capitalism' in Latin America between 1955 and 1965 (from Kubitschek to Goulard in Brazil or from Frondizi to Ilía in Argentina, and eventually to Onganía's coup of 1966) shows the inviability of peripheral capitalism. The pretence of aid in 'capital' and 'technology'

E

(confronting the 'capital' and 'technology' of poor and backward national capitalism) did not produce 'development', but implanted the 'transnational corporations' which increased the extraction of wealth (in economic terms 'profit', in theological terms the 'life' and 'blood' of the peoples and workers of the periphery).[22]

The *ethics of liberation* originated historically as a theoretical attempt (in theology and philosophy) to clarify a praxis which originated in the failure of 'developmentalism'.[23] Consequently, just as Karl Barth said of theology in general, 'The relation between such a God and such a man, and the relation between such a man and such a God, is for me the theme of the Bible and the essence of philosophy,'[24] to indicate the actual and existential nature of the relationship, for the ethics of liberation (and so for fundamental theology, as we shall see), the premise would be: The relationship of the *living* God with this *poor* person, and of this *poor* person with the *living* God, is what the Bible and theology are about. In this way we connect with, and continue on new foundations (no longer European and North American, but worldwide), the leading ideas of the 'early' Barth, Tillich, Niebuhr and so many others. But the theoretical connection is possible because there is a practical and historical connection. The Christians of the twenties and thirties opposed capitalism in crisis (and were buried by fascist capitalism in Europe and the United States). We too are opposing capitalism, but a capitalism in a crisis which is structural and much deeper, because autonomous national capitalism is now impossible at the periphery. The production of wealth in the underdeveloped countries of the periphery and its distribution to the vast impoverished majorities is impossible for capitalism. The ethics of liberation comes into being as a theory preceded and required by a praxis which opposes the system as a totality. Reformist 'developmentalism' puts forward—without success—alternative models (the varieties of 'developmentalism' represented by the UN Commission for Latin America, 'National Security', 'neo-populism', 'Christian democracy', and so on), but accepts the system as a whole. It is once more a moral system with 'norms', 'virtues' and 'values' as a basis. In contrast, the first task of the ethics of liberation is to de-base (to destroy the basis of) the system in order to arrive at another basis which transcends the present system. Analytic thought gives way to dialectical thought, and negative dialectics to the 'analectic' approach (affirmation as the origin of negation, as we shall see).

(a) 'Flesh' (totality)

Reformist moral systems ask themselves, 'How is it possible to be good *in* Egypt?' Their answers are in terms of norms, virtues, etc., but they accept Egypt as the system in force. Moses, on the other hand, asked himself, 'How is it possible to *get out of* Egypt?' But in order to get out,[25] I have to be aware that there is a totality within which I am and an 'outside' to which I can move. In other words, the *ethics* of liberation (in contrast to the 'intra-systemic' moral systems)[26] starts by describing the system within which the subject always starts, whether the practical subject (oppressor or oppressed) or the theoretical subject (the theologian himself). In the Bible the system as a totality is 'this world',[27] or the 'flesh' (*basár* in Hebrew and *sarx* in Greek), which is not to be confused with 'body' (*sóma* in Greek), though the two are sometimes confused in the Septuagint and Paul. The 'sin of the flesh' or the 'sin of Adam' is, precisely, idolatry, fetishism; it is treating the 'totality' as the ultimate, absolute totality and by so doing denying the existence of the other (Abel) and so of God (the absolute Other). The absolutisation of the totality is the sin of the flesh because there has *already* been a denial of the other in practice: 'Cain rose up against his brother Abel and killed him' (Gen. 4:8).

Today in Latin America, without making invalid connections, we can say that 'the system' is Anglo-Saxon capitalism in society, machismo in sexual attitudes, ideological domination in education: idolatry on every level. The idea has the inexhaustible profundity of reality, and in it is revealed the infinite human capacity to create 'systems' which may set themselves in opposition to God as idols.

(b) The 'other' (analectical exteriority)

Ethics, before dealing ontically with the range of moral problems, has to clarify the fact and the reality of the continued presence of the other 'beyond' any totality. *Totalité et Infini* has demonstrated this in phenomenological terms,[28] but not in terms of political economy.[29] Contrary to the charges of its critics, the ethics of liberation is not—in the Nietzschean echo—a 'Marxism for the people', but has firm roots in metaphysics (Xavier Zubiri rightly maintains in *Sobre la esencia* that reality transcends being), in an ethics as a first philosophy. This is a favourite remark of Levinas, and, as we shall see, a theological ethics is fundamental theology in its primary essence. 'Beyond' (*jenseits*), transcendental (ontologically transcendental), on the horizon of the system (of the flesh, of totality), 'the other' appears (as an 'epiphany' and not a mere 'phenomenon'), as a person who 'provokes' (calles—*vocare* in Latin—from in front—*pro* in Latin) and demands justice. The 'other' ('the widow, the orphan, the foreigner', in the prophets' formulation, or under the universal name of 'the poor person') confronting the system is the metaphysical *reality* beyond the ontological *being* of the system. As a result he or she is 'exteriority',[30] what is most alien to the system as a totality, 'internal transcendence', in F. Hinkelammert's phrase;[31] he or she is the 'locus' of God's epiphany, the poor person. *In* the system the only possible *locus* of God's epiphany is those who are non-system, what is other than the system, the poor. Jesus' identification with the poor (Matt. 25) is not a metaphor; *it is a logic*. God, the other absolute, is revealed in the flesh (the system) by what is other than the system, the poor. The metaphysical (and eschatological) exteriority of the poor, which is both theological and economic, in the sense of a 'theologal economy',[32] situates them as the key (historical) reality and (epistemological) category of the whole ethics of liberation (or of fundamental theology as such).

(c) Alienation, sin, oppression

In the system (the first element of the method and the first concept) the other (the second element, but the 'key', more radical than the first) *is alienated* (the third element and category). The 'alienation' of the 'other' (making it 'other' than itself) is, metaphysically making it 'the same', a mere functional part within the system. The human being, the living and free subject of creative labour, sells his labour and *becomes* a 'wage-earner', an intrinsic, ontic element of capitalism, dependent on the *being* of capital. The 'other' (who is free) becomes other than himself or herself, a thing. Just as Christ 'became other than himself and took the form of a servant',[33] so the 'other' becomes oppressed, 'poor' as a complex category (as exteriority and interiority dominated in the *flesh*). The 'poor person', as the one who does not enjoy the fruit of his or her labour, is the manifestation of sin *in the system*. Sin, which is simply domination-of-the-other, is revealed when someone is poor. The poor are the others stripped of their exteriority of their dignity, of their rights, of their freedom, and transformed into instruments for the ends of the dominator, the Lord, the Idol, the Fetish.

It is clear that the whole of this description is applicable to the social reality of exploited classes, oppressed countries, the sex which is violated, and so on, but this 'application' destroys the very foundations of the moral theologies current in Europe and North America. It starts by posing problems which cannot be 'conveniently' relegated to an appendix of ethico-social theology. Rather, since what is at issue is the very construction, the very *a priori* of the subjectivity which does theology—as a theory—and of Christian subjectivity in practice, they are the *primary* questions of all theology (as fundamental theology). The question, 'Is it possible to believe?' is preceded by the question, 'What are the practical and historical conditions of this question itself?' If I ask this question from the point of view of the 'Pharaonic class' in Egypt, it is not the same as if I ask it from the point of view of 'the slaves'. *From what position* am I now asking my first question in fundamental theology? This 'From what position?' in historical and social terms is the first chapter of *all theology*, and not an additional question in the section on 'alms': 'aid to under-developed countries'. We know that our colleagues of the 'centre' do not agree about this. The next few decades will tell us who is right.

(*d*) Liberation, salvation, 'going out'

Only in this 'fourth' (methodological and real) element is it possible to understand the question of redemption (Christology), as salvation (eschatology) and liberation. Each of these concepts says the same thing, but in relation to different terms. 'Liberation' implies a relation with a previous term (*ex quo*), from where? from prison. The 'prison' is at the same time (because *it is the same thing*) the system of oppression and sin. The concept (and the reality) of liberation includes two terms and one actuality (like the concept of movement): departure *from* somewhere, *to* somewhere, and the journey itself. Theologically, metaphorically and historically these terms are: from Egypt, to the promised land and the journey through the desert. The concept of 'freedom'—as in Häring's moral theology—does not have the same dialectical density or the historical complexity or the practical clarity of the category (and praxis) of liberation. The fact that Abraham, Moses and so many others 'depart' from the 'land' of Chaldea or Egypt for another 'land' 'which I shall show you',[34] sets up a dialectic between *two* terms. Because the current moral theologies (those mentioned before) do not radically question the first 'land' (the 'old man'; in Latin America the *present* system of oppression, today, is dependent capitalism), because they do not set up as the *necessary* horizon of *all* their discourse the utopia of the future 'land' (the 'new man'), everything they deal with in their treatises is reformist morality, in the land of the Chaldeans, in Egypt. They will never 'go out' into the desert, nor will they receive, in the desert, the 'new' law (the 'new' norms of morals).

The question of norms, laws, virtues, values and even ends must from the start be placed 'within' the problematic of the *two* lands (totality/exteriority, current system/utopia, dependent capitalism/alternatives, etc.). Consequently the question of an ethics *of liberation* (objective genitive) is that of how to be 'good' (just, saved), not in Egypt or in the monarchy under David, but in the journey of transition from an 'old' order to the 'new' order which is *not-yet* in force. The heroes and the saints do not guide their conduct by the 'current' norms. If they had, Washington would have remained a good subject of the English monarchs, the priest Hidalgo would have obeyed the Laws of the Spanish Indies, the heroes of the 'French resistance' would have submissively carried out Nazi commands in France, or Fidel Castro would have allowed Cuba to continue being a 'weekend' colony of the United States. What is the ethical basis of the praxis of the heroes when they rise against laws, rules, alleged virtues and values, against the ends of an *unjust* system? This question, which for Europeans and North Americans can occupy an appendix in moral theology, is for the Christians of the periphery the first chapter of any fundamental theology, since it answers the question 'What is theology *as a totality* for?' Barth, Tillich, Niebuhr, before the crisis of 1929, glimpsed these questions, but remained a long way from any possibility of dealing with them in a way adequate to the complexity of the world situation.

The ethics of liberation is a rethinking of the totality of moral problems from the point of view and the demands of 'responsibility' for the poor,[35] for a historical alternative which *allows struggle* in Egypt, a journey through the desert in the time of transition, and the building of the promised land. This promised land is the historical promised land which will always be judged by the eschatological land 'beyond any possibility of historical material production', the kingdom of heaven which will never be built *at all* in history, but which is already being built in the building of the lands which precede it in the same history.

3. A WORD ON METHOD

When one imagines (like Popper in *The Open Society and its Enemies*) that one has proved that any alternative social vision is a utopia, and that utopias are the root of all evil, the result in theology is an anti-utopian Christianity. It is then quite logical that the method of moral theology can only be analytic (in the tradition of Ayer, Wittgenstein, etc.),[36] more or less eclectic, taking something from sociology, from medicine, from politics, according to the branch of moral theology in question. These methods are valid, but provided they are treated as elements in a partial account of moral theology. They become ideological methods, methods which obscure reality, when they claim sole validity and when they criticise holistic methods as imprecise and unscientific.

Challenging the system as a whole is the characteristic of the dialectical method, from Plato or Aristotle,[37] via Thomas Aquinas, Kant, Hegel and Sartre. In reality, to use the language of Heidegger, whose concept of 'the world' is strictly dialectical, it is an attempt to situate ontologically every object or thing which appears to me ontically. Being ready to refer the means, the instrument, 'to the hand', the object to its basis (to being) is the characteristic of the dialectical method. In these terms, Marx is simply inquiring into commodities, money, production, etc. in the light of, in relation to the basis of the being of capital (the essence of capitalism). However, the ontological method, in this case an economic ontology,[38] has insisted on 'negation of the negation' or 'negative dialectic' (for example Adorno or the Frankfurt School, and even Ernst Bloch may be included). The revolutionary process, of negation of the totality in force (Lukács), is a praxis which arises out of the negation of the negation: out of the negation of the oppression produced by the system among the oppressed. In a sense, the negation of the negation has the system as its horizon and can only be transcended in terms of a utopia. This may be an artistic fantasy (Marcuse, *Eros and Civilisation*) or a future alternative, but in fact it is a possibility in terms of 'the same' system. The origin of the negation is either the same system or an empty horizon (pure possibility or transcendent horizon: the kingdom of freedom as absolute free time).

The ethics of liberation, in contrast, starts from the affirmation of the real, existing, historical other. We have called this trans-ontological (metaphysical) positive element of the impetus, this active starting point of the negation of the negation, *the analectic element*. The Greek prefix *ana-* is meant to indicate a 'going beyond' the ontological horizon (the system, the 'flesh').[39] This *logos* (*ana-logos*), a discourse which has its origin in the transcending of the system, contains the originality of the Hebrew-Christian experience. If 'in the beginning God created' (Gen 1:1), it is because the Other is prior to the very principle of the cosmos, the system, the 'flesh'. The metaphysical priority of the other (who creates, reveals himself or herself) also has historical, political and erotic elements. The poor, the oppressed class, the nation on the periphery, the woman treated as a sexual object, have *reality* 'beyond' the limits of the system which alienates, represses and dehumanises them. The 'reality' which the people of Nicaragua embodied, 'beyond' the limits of the Somoza regime and dependent capitalism, is the basis for a negation of oppression and the motivation for a practice of liberation. The oppressed contain (in the structure of their subjectivity, of their culture, of their underground economy, etc., in their analectic exteriority) the trans-systematic (eschatological) impulse which enables them to discover themselves as oppressed *in the system*. They discover themselves 'as oppressed' if they make attempts to be (eschatologically) other than the system in their exteriority to it. The analectical affirmation of their dignity and freedom (which is negated in the system), of their culture, of their labour, outside the system is the source of the very mobility of the dialectic. (They affirm what is 'unproductive labour' for capital, but real in its own terms, and affirm it outside the system, not because the poor have conquered the system, but frequently because the system considers them 'nothing', non-being; and it is out of this (real) nothingness that new systems are built.)

The method, and historical reality, does not begin with the negation of oppression, but negation of oppression begins with the analectical affirmation of the (historical and eschatological) exteriority of the other, through whose project of liberation the negation of the negation and the building of new systems is put into effect. These new systems are not simply univocal results of the actualisation of what was present potentially in the old unjust system. The new system is an analogical realisation which includes something of the old system (*similitudo*) and something absolutely new (*distinctio*). The new system was impossible for the old one; there is creation in the bursting in of the analectical otherness of the poor in their own liberation.[40] The method of the ethics of liberation is analectic, because it is an element in the creative action of the unconditioned freedom of God and in the redemptive act of the subsumption in Christ of the flesh (the system) by the analectic irruption of the Word, the negation of sin and the building of the kingdom. There is not merely a negative dialectic, but also a positive dialectic in which the exteriority of the other (the creator, Christ, the poor person) is the positive practical condition of the very movement of the method. Consequently the poor, and their own liberating praxis, are, as an analectical priority, the fundamental and initial element. The ethics comes afterwards, affirming as its first premise the absolute priority of the poor person, this poor person in whom we encounter, as an absolute challenge and responsibility, Christ, a poor person who is God himself.

In Latin America an ethics of liberation must justify the goodness, heroism and holiness of an oppressed people's action for liberation in El Salvador, Guatemala, Argentina or Brazil (in Egypt), of a people already journeying through the desert (as in Nicaragua) where 'Aaron the priest', wanting to return to Egypt, pays homage to the golden calf (the idol), while the prophet (Moses: the ethics of liberation?) has not only to destroy the fetish, but also to offer to the people who are liberating themselves the 'new' law. But the new law is born in dialectical opposition to the law in Egypt. It is not possible to begin by defining—as moral theologies do—the morality of an action by its transcendental relation to a norm or law. On the contrary, the absolute morality of the action indicates its transcendental relation to the building of the kingdom in the historical processes of the liberation of actual material peoples, 'who are hungry'. It is only subsequently, within this framework, that it becomes possible to situate all the problems of abstract moral subjectivity (with which all moral theologies start).

The publication of the encyclical *Laborem exercens* has given us a good foundation on which to build an ethics of liberation in the exploited flesh of poor workers, a eucharistic or economic radicalism which must be developed in the future.[41]

Notes

1. See Paul Tillich, 'The Social Function of the Churches in Europe and America' *Social Research* 3, 1 (New York 1936), and (in German) in *Gesammelte Werke* III (Stuttgart 1962) pp. 107ff. Tillich says: 'I know that the social functions of the churches cannot be fully understood without considering their social structure and their economic basis and examining the social order to which they belong' (translated from the German, p. 119).

2. It is impossible for the author not to remember 30th March 1975, when he was included in

similar lists and expelled from the 'National University of Cuyo' for similar reasons, and many other cases in Latin America.

3. Hitler's 'Nazism' was a right-wing government which made German *national* capitalism (Krupp, Thiessen, Siemens, etc.) viable and staked a claim for the world domination of the capitalist market. The military governments of Latin America (since 1964) have been ensuring the viability of a capitalism dependent on the USA, which is much worse.

4. Prologue to vol. II of his *Gesammelte Werke, Christentum und soziale Gestaltung* (1919–33), p. 11.

5. New York 1932.

6. (London 1937). Original: *Das Gebot und die Ordnungen* (Tübingen 1932).

7. See the work cited in note 5, at p. 277. The book is 'a social analysis which is written, at least partially, from the perspective of a disillusioned generation' (p. XXV). 'In Germany E. Bernstein . . . changed the expectations of catastrophe into hope of evolutionary progress towards equal justice' (p. 181).

8. Eng. ed. New York 1977. Original in *Gesammelte Werke* II.

9. See C. Howard Hopkins *The Rise of the Social Gospel in American Protestantism (1865–1915)* (New Haven 1940); Robert Handy *The Social Gospel in America 1870–1920* (Oxford 1966); Aaron Abell *American Catholicism and Social Action 1865–1950* (Garden City, New York 1960).

10. Boston 1893, pp. 275ff.

11. *Ibid.*, p. 275.

12. At pp. 257ff. there is a discussion on the concept of value in Marx (50 years before the publication of the 1844 manuscripts, which accounts for some naive misrepresentations). At one point he asks, 'We go part way with Marx and Robertus; then we part company with them. How far can we wisely go with them? How many of their projects may we safely adopt?' (p. 280). 'Socialism, as we have seen, is simply a proposition to extend the functions of the State so that it shall include and control nearly all the interests of life (sic). Now, I take it, we are agreed that, as Christians, we have a right to make use of the power of the State, both in protecting life and property, and in promoting, to some extent, the general welfare' (p. 281). This was written in the US in 1893. What happened afterwards? The working-class movement was brutally repressed (see James Weinstein, *The Decline of Socialism in America 1912–1925* (Boston 1967).

13. *Christianizing the Social Order* (New York 1919), pp. 222ff.

14. See for example Bernhard Häring, *Free and Faithful in Christ. Moral Theology for Priests and Laity*, 3 vols. (Slough 1978–1981). Though much better than other Catholic moral theologians, Häring nevertheless treats as subsidiary questions of economic and political ethics (vol. III, ch. VII, pp. 244–325), and discusses 'life' solely in relation to medical matters and abortion (vol. III, pp. 4–113, not with work or social life (repression of the poor, etc.).
Similarly in the *Handbuch der christlichen Ethik*, ed. A. Hertz, W. Korff, T. Rendtorff and H. Ringeling, 3 vols. (Freiburg 1978–1982), the main problem is 'modernity', and the first moral topic is 'rules' (vol. I, pp. 108ff.). 'Life' has to do only with medicine. Politics is defined in terms of 'the principles of constitutional government' (vol. II, pp. 215ff.). There is a little on economics, but under the title (directed at the peripheral countries) 'Aid' (II, pp. 417ff.). The 'new international order' is given no biblical, ontological or anthropological basis, but defended solely on sociological grounds (III, pp. 337ff.).

15. Chapters 34 ('The Nature and the Task of the Economic Order') and 35 ('The Christian in the Present Economic Order'), pp. 395ff. The quotation is from p. 426 (translated slightly amended).

16. *Ibid.*, pp. 426ff. For the author the Christian position is a sort of social democratic 'third way' (pp. 431ff.).

17. (Tübingen), esp. vol. II/2 (1958). He leaves the problem of property to a separate appendix (vol. III, 1964, pp. 224ff.), showing a sort of 'economic blindness'. His analyses are exclusively in legal or socio-political terms. There is an abridged English edition of vols. I–II, *Theological Ethics*, 2 vols. (London and Philadelphia 1968–1969). Vol. II of the English corresponds to vol. II/2 of the German.

18. English ed., II, pp. 341–343.

19. See Jürgen Habermas 'Die Kulturkritik der Neokonservativen in den USA und in der Bundesrepublik' *Praxis*, II, 4 (1983), pp. 339 ff. See also Habermas's book *Theorie des kommunikativen Handelns* (Frankfurt 1981), but here he does not deal at all with the question of the peripheral countries—though it is intimately connected with that of 'instrumental reason'.

20. Philadelphia 1981, p. 174. Take the case of Michael Novak, who, after beginning his career as a liberal Catholic theologian with *The Open Church* (1964) and *The Men who make the Council* (1964), went on to write *Toward a Theology of the (transnational) Corporation* (1981), published by the American Enterprise Institute, and *The Spirit of Democratic Capitalism* (1982). These neo-conservative theologies are not 'economically blind': 'The official documents of the popes and the Protestant ecumenical bodies are notably strong on moral vision, much less so in describing economic principles and realities. The coming generation will inherit as a task the need to create and to set forth systematically a theology of economics' (Novak 1981, p. 21).

21. At p. 174.

22. See my article 'The Bread of the Eucharistic Celebration as a Sign of Justice in the Community' *Concilium* 152 (1982) 56, where I demonstrate the relationship between life, blood, labour and production. A 'theology of money' and of the economy must start from these metaphysical and biblical postulates (see *zao*, 'life', 'live', in Kittel, TDNT II, pp. 832–875 (Bultmann and Bertram).

23. The disparaging term 'developmentalism' is meant to indicate the ideological and false character of the European and North American 'doctrine of development' (and of 'development aid') which dominates in Christian (and United Nations) circles. This is an attempt to provide a partial remedy for *effects*, aggravates the problem and does not attack the structural and global *causes* of the 'crisis'.

24. *The Epistle to the Romans*, 6th ed. (London, Oxford, New York 1968) p. 10.

25. The concept of 'going out', 'being brought out' (Gen. 21:1; Exod. 13:16, etc.) is a fundamental theological metaphor.

26. On the difference between 'morality' and 'ethics' see the end of this article in *Para una ética de la liberación latinoamericana*, Siglo XXI (Buenos Aires 1973), II, 20 (2nd ed., Mexico 1977, vol. II, p. 13), and 'One Ethic and Many Moralities' in *Concilium* 150 (1980) 54.

27. See *Para una ética de la liberación (EL)*, II, sect. 21, pp. 22ff. On the category of 'flesh' or 'totality', see *EL*, chs. 1–2 (I, pp. 33ff.); *El humanismo semita* (Buenos Aires 1969); *El dualismo en la antropolgía de la cristianidad* (Buenos Aires 1974); *History and Theology of Liberation* (New York 1976) ch. 1, etc.

28. The title of a book by Emmanuel Levinas *Totalité et Infini. Essai sur l'exteriorité* (The Hague 1961).

29. For my view on Levinas, see *Emmanuel Levinas y la liberación latinoamericana* (Buenos Aires 1975) prologue.

30. In *Filosofía da Libertação*, 2.4 (pp. 45ff.); *EL* I, ch. III, pp. 97ff.; III, ch. VII, sect. 46, pp. 97ff.; *ibid.*, sect. 52, pp. 168ff.; IV, ch. IX, sect. 65, pp. 94ff.; V, ch. X, sect. 72, pp. 76ff.

31. *Las armas ideológicas de la muerte* (San Jose 1977) p. 61: 'Praxis is directed towards a transcendence within real, material life. It is a vision of community full of this real life without its negativity.'

32. See the article cited in note 22 above.

33. It is known that Luther translated the Greek of Phil. 2:7 by *äusserte sich*, 'dispossessed himself', a term characteristic of 'kenotic' theology, from where it came down to Hegel through his professors of Christology at Tübingen. It is a fundamental Christian concept.

34. The category 'land' (*'arets*) has a strict eschatological sense in the Bible. See Kittel TWNT I, 676, art. *ge*, 'earth'. This sense is present in Ps. 37:11; Matt. 5:5 and Heb. 11:9. Here, however I want to show the dialectic between the two lands: '. . . from the land (*me'aretskha*) . . . to the land (*'el-ha'rets*) which I shall show you' (Gen. 12:1); 'out of that land to a good and broad land, flowing with milk and honey' (Exod. 3.8). It is a going 'out of Egypt' (*mi-mitsraim*, Exod. 3.10).

35. 'Responsibility' *for the other*, for the oppressed, *in the face of* the actual oppressive economic system (Hans Jonas *Das Prinzip Verantwortung*, Frankfurt 1982, does not give the contextual

meaning of 'responsibility', which remains at an abstract level. He considers 'technology', but never as an element 'of capital' (*als Kapital*). He does not understand this 'subsumption').

36. See *Handbuch der christlichen Ethik*, vol. I, pp. 68ff., F. Boeckle's contribution ('Der sprachanalytische Ansatz', etc.).

37. See my *Método para una filosofía de la liberación* (Salamanca 1974).

38. Marx's *Grundrisse* and, more recently, the manuscripts of 1861–1863, authorise us to reinterpret Marx in terms of an ontology in the strict sense: K. Marx *Grundrisse* (London 1973); *Zur Kritik der politischen Oekonomie (Manuskripte 1861–1863)*, MEGA III/2, vols. I–VI (Berlin 1977–1982: 'Capital thus becomes a very mysterious creature,' p. 2163, line 11).

39. See my recent article on 'analectic', 'Pensée analectique en philosophie de la libération' *Analogie et Dialectique* (Geneva 1982), pp. 93–120.

40. *EL* sect. 25, vol. II, pp. 58ff.; sect. 47, vol. III, pp. 109ff; sect. 66, vol. IV, pp. 109ff; sect. 73, vol. V, pp. 91ff.

41. Polish thinkers have rightly taken 'labour' as the centre of theological reflection (see Josef Tischner *La svolta storica* (Bologna 1982), esp. 'Il lavoro privo di senso', pp. 76ff). For the Poles the problem is control of the product of labour by the producer. For Latin America the problem is the consumption (why there is a hunger as a result of oppression and structural theft) of the product of labour. In Poland the workers (the nation) want to know why they are producing bread, and want control of their production. In Latin America the nation (the people) want to possess the fruits of their work, the eucharistic bread. See John Desrochers *The Social Teaching of the Church* (Bangalore 1982), esp. pp. 637ff. It is clear that *Laborem exercens* allows the ethics of liberation to sharpen its agruments considerably.

PART III

Towards a Dialogue between the Ethic of Autonomy and the Ethic of Liberation

Luise Schottroff

Experiences of Liberation Liberty and Liberation According to Biblical Testimony

1. BONDAGE

THE WORD 'freedom' has its historical roots in one of the cruellest inventions in a human history anything but lacking in brutality. 'Freemen' were the people with full civic rights who let others work for them as bondsmen or slaves. In the eyes of these people, slaves ('unfree' in the legal sense) were 'animated property', 'tools'. Since we who are free cannot dispense with slave labour, this must be nature's design, says Aristotle, formulating the subjective viewpoint of freemen in the ancient world (*Politica* 1253 b 30; 1252 a 30). The realities of slavery are appositely described in the 'slave' parables in the gospels. True, slaves do not go hungry, for their owners have an interest in their working capacity; but their everyday lives take their very definition from the experience of violence. They are tortured, beaten, and put to death. There is violence among the slaves themselves too. Slaves hit one another and report their fellow-slaves to their masters (Matt. 22:6; 21.35f.; 24:51, 18:31; Luke 12:45).

The Bible depicts the slave's servitude; but it describes too the peasant's lack of personal freedom and the political bondage of whole nations; for all this reflects the social reality of biblical times. The peasant population of Palestine in the early years of Christianity was not enslaved in the legal sense, but it was ground down by debt. The situation of the debtor unable to pay, and face to face with his creditor's power, is a continually repeated scene which was the nightmare of many people (see e.g. Neh. 5:1–5; Luke 12:58f.). It is not by chance that it was this situation which offered the obvious image for God's forgiveness. To say that God forgives means that he excuses debts (see Matt. 6:12ff.; 18:23–35). The little farmer with his load of debt was faced with the prospect of having his clothing taken in pledge, his family sold, imprisonment or serfdom for debt, destitution and sickness—at best the life of a day-labourer, who had to endure long periods of unemployment. The picture which the gospels give of the situation of the farming population at the time is realistic, and frequently authenticated by non-Christian sources. The New Testament also describes the political bondage of whole nations in the bluntest terms: 'You know that those who count as masters over the nations subjugate them, and misuse their power' (Mark 10:42).

Romans 13:1–7 belongs to a whole series of declarations of submission made by oppressed nations to their political rulers. Christians, Jews, and other politically subjugated peoples made declarations of loyalty to the Romans of just the kind we find in Rom. 13:1–7, for example; and yet they knew that political conflict was unavoidable as long as they put their God above the gods of their political masters.

Like most educated people in the ancient world, Plato and Aristotle talk about freedom from the perspective of 'freemen'—which meant the prosperous, 'the lords and masters' of the rest. But the biblical traditions see things from the angle of the underdogs. In the Bible we do not find freemen talking about the way they see themselves, or Stoic philosophers discoursing on inward liberty. The Bible is always conscious of the viewpoint of the people whose experience is bounded by the three walls of enslavement, impoverishment and death, as well as by political oppression. It is not chance that we find no biblical analogies for the ideas of Aristotle we have described. In Seneca, for example (*De beneficiis* III, 20, 1) we find the concept of an inward liberty, attainable in spite of outward conditions. But this is not a biblical idea; and it is not Pauline either, though some commentators have so interpreted 1 Cor. 7:21f. (e.g. J. Weiss, in his comment on the passage). The notion of an inner liberty, independent of whether people are in fact hungry, or enslaved, or it may be prosperous, belongs to the situation of a wealthy class which sees its opportunities for political action restricted (see Seneca). But the Bible speaks with the voice of people marked by the experiences of subjection.

Lack of freedom—like freedom—is always understood in the Bible *as a whole*. The New Testament word 'body' (σῶμα) expresses this totality: servitude is bodily, psychological, social and religious reality. All sectors of human identity are affected—even hopes are destroyed (we only have to look at Rom. 6:12–14). The inner life and outward conditions are not separated, and the physical sufferings of bondage are exactly described (see e.g., 1 Cor. 4:11–13, or the accounts of the passion of Christ, whose death belongs together with the execution of many people in a comparable situation).

Lack of liberty in all areas of life is not reported without inferences: it is clearly censured. Political repression is something frightful (see above for the phrases used in Mark 10:42). Paul also assumes that Roman government is an unjust rule, which has been established by God. The tyranny of masters over slaves, Greeks over barbarians, and men over women is unjust in the eyes of God as well—that is the clear premise underlying Gal. 3:28 and 1 Cor. 12:13. The parables in the gospels, too, which compare God with a creditor or wealthy landowner are not on the creditor's or landowner's side. They show what the wrath of God is like. People who have dealt mercilessly with their fellows stand before the angry God as the debtor who is unable to pay stands before the creditor, with his total power over the trembling little man in front of him. Lack of liberty characterises the world of slaves, tenant-farmers and day-labourers; and it is a world naked and open for the wrath of God. The everyday experiences of society as it is, show that where men and women are concerned God's creation has been shattered.

The essential point about the Bible's description of servitude is that it is depicted *from the angle of people who have escaped*. The exodus from slavery in Egypt becomes the heart of a people's experience of God—a people sustained by the remembrance of that past liberation whenever it is weighed down by new oppression (Deut. 24:18, 22; 15:15, and frequently elsewhere). In the New Testament too, oppression is described from the perspective of liberation, and is therefore only perceived at all in its comprehensive structure. It is only as someone who has been liberated, in whom the Spirit of God dwells, that Paul can say how hard the imprisonment of sin really was (Rom. 7:25; see also 8:1). The Gospel of the poor—which Jesus and the Jesus movement saw as the fulfilment of the divine promise (Isa. 61:1)—brings the liberation which makes people capable of perceiving the wholesale havoc which poverty causes. It is not only hunger, weeping and sickness that crush the poor so utterly; it is the inability to praise God, so that they are poor 'in spirit'—poor to the very core (Matt. 5:3).

The Bible therefore sees lack of liberty mainly in three sectors: the oppression of slaves, the oppression of debtors and the oppression of nations. But in a wider context still we discover a marked sensitivity towards the brutality involved in the lordship of one human being over another, and also towards violence in the relationship of men to women. Here the relationships of power are seen from the angle of the people affected. They are seen as a whole, in their all-embracing structure, and they are detested as injustice in the face of God. The biblical tradition describes lack of liberty so radically because the people involved had already experienced liberation—already had one foot on liberated ground.

2. THE JESUS MOVEMENT:
THE SOVEREIGN RULE OF GOD AS PROCESS OF LIBERATION

It is only on the fringe of the synoptic gospels (Matt. 17:26) that we meet the word liberty (ἐλευθερία etc.) and its cognates. But it can be useful to use the word 'liberation' to translate and bring out the meaning of other words—for example, forgiveness, or release (ἄφεσις), which is used to describe the remittance of debts, the freeing of prisoners, and God's forgiveness, The beatitude is also an expression of liberation, just like the word 'gospel'. The good news of the Gospel means that the misery of the poor is at an end. The beatitude is not merely the promise of a future; it already brings about the beginning of God's rule in the present (we only have to look at Matt. 5:3ff., comparing it with Matt. 11:5ff.). We therefore have to understand the expression about God's kingdom as being itself a term for liberation; and we have to see the history of Jesus and his disciples in New Testament times, not only as the history of people who proclaimed liberation, but also as the history of actual liberation practice, in which other people were involved as well as Jesus, and which lived on after his death.

God is king; he is the Lord of the whole creation: this already means liberation, now: 'No one can serve two masters, . . . you cannot serve God and mammon' (Matt. 6:24). The kingdom of God ends the oppression of the rule of men and their gods, mammon and the rest. God's rule is the counter-force of One who is mightier still, against the might which deprives people of their liberty. Oppression by political masters and oppression by demons is on the same level and is dangerous and all-embracing.

The liberating practice of Jesus meant that people gathered together in the community of his people. From the very beginning, Jesus' followers formed communities, living together and wandering through the country together. The account in Acts (2:42–47) about the first congregation in Jerusalem after Jesus' resurrection probably gives us an accurate description of all the essential elements of the form this community took. Common prayer and shared joys (see below), common meals, sharing of their scanty food, healing of the sick. The misery of disease was widespread in that poverty-stricken country. In the villages and towns of Palestine the sick were to be met with in the market place, or at the public sanctuaries for sick people, like the pool of Bethesda (John 5:4; Luke 10:9 and frequently). Jesus and his followers healed the sick and everyone involved saw these healings as the beginning of the liberation of the whole Jewish people. The liberating practice of Jesus spread at an astonishing rate. Everyone was to be reached. Anyone who was healed immediately became healer and prophet himself. The new communities did not close themselves against the outside world. They were consistently concerned to appeal publicly to every individual person, as well as to whole towns and villages, in a way people could understand. The kingdom of God is an all-embracing goal, because God is the Lord and Creator of the whole world. Out of this purpose emerged practical ways of behaviour for people in the discipleship of Jesus. Even the conflicts which grew out of the practice of liberation were endured in the light of the comprehensive objective. Believers proclaimed the imminent judgment of God on everyone who committed injustice against God and other people. But the proclamation of judgment left punishment to God. The very clearness of the confrontation with the will of God was intended to win every enemy of Jesus' message: perhaps he would still repent (Matt. 5:44f.)! The difficulties with which the Jesus movement, like Jesus himself, had to struggle, were great; and, like Jesus, many of his messengers were put to death because of their work. It was hard for all concerned to endure the all-too-justifiable fear. The account of the passion in Mark's Gospel brings out this fear very clearly. All the disciples fled (Mark 14:50) because they had reason to be afraid that, as Jesus' supporters, they would be arrested and crucified like him. The leaders of the Jewish people co-operated with the Romans who were, practically speaking, the political rulers. Their purpose was to stamp immediately on all popular unrest. The Jesus movement was not a political movement, in the sense of having a political goal, such as the expulsion of the Romans. But since its aim was to transform the whole nation into children of God, serving God only, and no other master, it presented a massive threat to the *de facto* power. The day could be foreseen when the people would take their bearings from God, and no longer from mammon—a day when they would no longer be ill-treated and oppressed 'like sheep without a shepherd' (Matt. 9:36).

The transformation of men and women from slaves to freemen meant becoming a child of God. Generally, however, in accordance with the patriarchalism of the time, people talked about becoming 'a son of God' (see for example Matt. 5:9; 5:45). To be God's sons or his children meant no longer being the slave of other masters and powers. It meant being capable of the love of children for one another, capable of experiencing the happiness of liberation as endowment with power. People in the discipleship of Jesus felt completely strong and victorious, not small and insignificant. There are numerous texts which express this sense of victory—for example, the parable of the mustard seed (Mark 4:30–32), or Mark 9:23: 'All things are possible to him who believes.' Being a child of God was another word for liberty. (On the connection between the status of child and the status of freeman see e.g. Matt: 17.26; John 8:33, 35.)

3. LIBERATION FROM THE POWER OF SIN

For Paul, liberty and 'making free' are important words. Paul's fundamental idea here is that, through Christ's resurrection, believers are freed from the power of sin (see especially Rom. 8:2; 6:18–22). Unfortunately, because of the way it has been used in the past, the word 'sin' is often misinterpreted in a moralistic, individualistic sense. But in Paul's view it is a power that rules in the world. Sin is a queen that dominates the whole of humanity and human history. The many great wrongs and petty meannesses which people do to one another (see e.g. the impressive list in Rom. 1:29–32) add up to a collective and compulsive system to which every individual is subjected. People are sold under sin, slaves to sin, unfree in all their vital impulses. The result, for individuals and humanity as a whole, is death. Rom. 7:14–24 describes the despairing situation of a humanity that has become the puppet of its collective drive towards self-destruction. Even the will of God, the Torah, which aims to make life possible for men and women, becomes the instrument of Queen Sin. She makes use of the Torah against its intention, and so the holy will of God practically signs the death warrant of men and women, since they are incapable of living according to that will. Christ's resurrection has ended this tyranny, says Paul. The power of sin has been broken, people can live under the protection of Christ, and do not have to work for death and destruction. Paul thinks of the power of God and the power of Christ as a great space in which people can live (that is why he talks about being 'in Christ', for example). It is a space which gives the protection out of which liberation from the power of sin can be experienced, in the form of a totally changed life.

Paul's ideas (and practical Christian life in the Pauline congregations) are by no means very different from those of the Jesus movement, as we know it from the synoptic gospels. The terminological differences are often unjustly stressed, without recognition of the practical points in common. Here too, the essential point is that believers live together in communities, and that their process of liberation takes its bearings from the goal of the sovereignty of God. Equality among themselves, love within the congregation, and the struggle to win people—every individual person—with the aim of reaching the whole of humanity: these things determined Christian behaviour.

The admonitions in Rom. 12:1–21 give us valuable insight into the mode of the Christian life—'worship in everyday life', to use the phrase in which Käsemann sums up the ideas in Rom. 12:1ff. (see E. Käsemann *New Testament Questions of Today*, Eng. trans. London 1969, pp. 188ff.). In Paul too the lordship of God and the lordship of Christ are understood as a *counter*-force. Liberation means putting oneself under the banner of the power of God, which is greater than what it opposes. In Rom. 6:19 Paul even considered the repellent aspects of this idea, undoubtedly finding it a problem that liberation can appear to be a new form of bondage—or so one might put it, without much exaggeration. Paul explains this by saying that the enslavement to sin, which has power over people's bodies, needs a counter-force ('just as . . . so', Rom. 6:19), which now makes these bodies capable of being sanctified, and able to 'bear fruit'.

Paul's views on slavery and the position of women in the Church has been the cause of much confusion. Generally, people start from the idealistic notion that Paul ought fundamentally to have demanded the end of slavery. Or we are told that he thought that the outward conditions of life were of secondary importance, therefore demanding that slaves should remain slaves. Both interpretations—of 1 Cor 7:21f. especially—display too little understanding of conditions of life at the time. The people who were unfree by law were only one section of the exploited population; the broad proletariat of day-labourers and freed slaves were certainly free in the legal sense, but in actual fact they were merely exploited with different methods. At this period it could be quite sensible procedure for a slave-owner to free a slave, and to continue to exploit him by way of services and through financial obligations. The difference in the lack of liberty enjoyed by a slave, a freed slave and a day-labourer (like Paul himself) was really quite relative. It is therefore important to see that the change in the situation of slaves in the Christian congregations was a *practical* change. They had the same rights as their fellow-Christians, and the congregations also expressed views on the relations between slave-owners and their slaves (as the Epistle to Philemon testifies). That is to say, they did not see the relationship of power between master and slave as the owner's personal affair. It was the *practical* nature of this change which, in the social context, gave the impression that this was an attack on 'the social order'. H. Thyen urges convincingly (in F. Crüsemann and H. Thyen *Als Mann und Frau geschaffen*, Gelnhausen 1978, pp. 158f.) that the proper translation of 1 Cor. 7:21 is Luther's: 'But if you can be freed, all the better for you,' (cf. RSV: 'But if you can gain your freedom, avail yourself of the opportunity')—the point being that emancipation evidently brought about merely a very questionable improvement in the situation.

In 1 Cor. 11:2–16, Paul expends considerable theological effort on justifying the woman's subordination to the man. But this precept does not reflect the *de facto* equality of women in the churches, even as prophetic proclaimers of the message (we only have to look at Rom. 16:1–16). However, here we cannot spare Paul the reproach of falling short of his own theory (Gal. 3:28) and the practice of the Christian congregations.

These congregations translated liberation from the power of sin into the practice of equality and love. Here Paul evidently had the distinct hope that the liberation of God's children would actually bring about the liberation of the whole creation, even nature (Rom. 8:21). In the eyes of Rome's administrators, the churches were perhaps small and still unimportant; but in the eyes of Paul they possessed the power to change the world.

F

4. THE SPIRIT, PRAYER AND LIBERTY

The Spirit of God is given to every believer (see e.g. 1 Cor. 12:13; Acts 2:13, 17) and means a fundamental change in his whole existence, since he has now escaped from the compulsive law of sin. The eighth chapter of Romans makes the connection between liberation and the Holy Spirit especially clear. The Spirit endows people with a new language—the language of prayer. They became capable of expressing their relation to God as his children, which is what their liberation means. When the believer is overwhelmed by the tremendous opportunities which now face him, the Spirit intercedes for him. So in the language of prayer God's perfect future—which means the perfect liberation of the whole creation—already becomes reality. Paul has a great vision: the whole creation is suffering the labour pains of liberation. Every word of prayer, every cry filled with the Spirit, is the first cry of the newly born creation. It is a stammering declaration of solidarity with all created things, which wait longingly for liberation (Rom. 8:15–27). Many expressions of the Spirit in the early Christian congregations may seem alien to us today, yet in their sensory and bodily expression they are fundamental experiences of liberation. The assembled congregation experiences its newly conferred power and the happiness of the escaped prisoner as something so convulsive that even the floor shakes, as Luke reports (Acts 4:31).

The Spirit of God fills people with power which makes them able to heal the sick and to speak openly and fearlessly (παρρησία). Believers were particularly frightened at the prospect of having to make a confession of their faith during official interrogations. They were afraid that words would fail them—that they would not know what to say. This was the hour of the Spirit. People comforted themselves with the thought that the Spirit himself would speak in this hour of need (Mark 13:11). This makes it understandable that even interrogations were efficacious as a central opportunity for proclamation. People who were generally speaking uneducated, though well-versed in the Bible, overcame their fear and spoke the truth: Christ is risen and there is no longer any ruler in the world but God.

Being changed by the Spirit also meant endowment with the capacity for joy and happiness. The parable of the Prodigal Son (Luke 15:11–32) brings out particularly well the different nuances of this aspect of the new existence. People are united in their joy over the end of the wretchedness of lost children. The feast of joy can really only be celebrated when no one is outside any longer. All the gifts of the Spirit establish a link between God's child and God himself; but they also forge a link between person and person—and not only people belonging to the Christian community. Anyone who has come to know the joy of liberation cannot rest until he sees that this liberty is spreading. The believer finds himself permanently in the situation of the Father at the end of the parable of the Prodigal Son: he stands outside and 'woos' the elder son, who does not see that he belongs. The persuasive power of the Christian faith in its early days was great. God punishes the person who commits an injustice: this was certainly clearly stated. But enthusiastic attempts were nevertheless made to win the person himself. For to love one's enemy was to imitate the God who is lord over the whole creation.

We can deduce from Pauline texts especially that endowment with the Spirit also led to an exuberance which Paul himself viewed as exaggerated and ruthless. In the question about meat offered to idols, some people no longer wanted to be ruled by any caution in cultic matters. In the ancient world, nearly all meat was slaughtered in the context of the cult. So to buy and eat meat inevitably meant participation in that cult. Paul says that we would certainly be free to ignore this caution, and our anxiety about being contaminated by alien cultic practices: after all, these cults have no religious significance for us. But there are people with whom we are closely associated who find this too difficult to accept; and we have to consider them (1 Cor. 10:29). So we have to forgo some newly acquired opportunities for the sake of other people (see also 1 Cor. 9:1, 12, 15).

The Spirit of God in believers made them all equal, for it was always one and the same spirit, and the quality of that Spirit never varied (see e.g. 1 Cor. 12:4–11). The very attempts which the Christian congregations made to translate the equality of believers into practice show what resistance was involved in the new life, in terms of everyday living. Society in the ancient world was hierarchically organised, and this hierarchy penetrated every human relationship. 'But it shall not be so among you' (Mark 10:43). But the question put by the sons of Zebedee (Mark 10:43), like 1 Cor. 12, shows that it is not easy to live out equality, even in a small congregation, in a hierarchical society built up on relationships of power. Different ideas and practice could not be developed from one day to the next, simply through a resolve. So in New Testament times, Christians found a radical solution to the problem. They said that everyone had to serve (διακονεῖν) in the lowest place. In the ancient world, the word *diakonia* meant the role of whoever came bottom in the hierarchy—slaves, children or women. Practical equality only exists where human relationships based on power end (Mark 10:42–45; see Rom. 12:16).

The process of liberation takes place where people 'at the bottom' organise their lives with the power of the divine Spirit. The powerful continually claim that they are liberating the powerless. But the result is only servitude, because the mighty cannot distinguish justice from injustice. Only those affected can do this—and God, who is on their side. This was the experience of Christianity in its early years.

Dominique Stein

Is the Psychoanalytic Experience an Experience of Autonomy?

1. WHAT IS THE PLACE OF AUTONOMY IN THE CONDITIONS UNDER WHICH THE PSYCHOANALYTIC CORPUS OF THEORY AND PRACTICE IS ACTUALLY PRODUCED?

IS THE psychoanalytic experience based on the exercise of autonomy? Is the point of psychoanalysis the winning of autonomy on the part of the subject who commits him/herself to psychoanalytic therapy? If one takes the conceptions of autonomy and de-alienation (or appropriation of identity) as synonymous and if one considers that neurotic inhibitions are major causes of alienation or oppression, one can give a first—albeit a crudely approximate—answer: Yes, psychoanalytic therapy has got something to do with a process of winning autonomy.

That, however, is only a first step. And if he goes on to ponder the moral and juridical, and therefore the historical and political connotations of the concept of autonomy (i.e. the right to govern oneself by one's own laws, to be one's own lawgiver), the psychoanalyst cannot avoid asking a number of questions of ever-increasing topicality about the way his practice and theory relate to the actual way in which that practice and theory come about, the *conditions of production*. The fact is that psychoanalytic therapy unfolds behind closed doors between the analyst and the patient, and yet the psychoanalyst has a history: he belongs (or refuses to belong) to a psychoanalytical society, and in any case she or he has been a patient who has committed her/himself to personal psychoanalytic therapy (a therapy that a growing number of analysts refuse to call a training analysis). It is therefore clear that every psychoanalytic situation *ipso facto* implies a process of formation of the psychoanalyst and a process of transmission of the practice and theory of psychoanalysis. This means that however private and individual the therapy may seem to be, it carries some minimal practico-theoretical reference to the initial, originating work of Freud and to the nexus of history in which any particular psychoanalyst is placed by virtue of his psychoanalytic genealogy. A claim to complete independence of the conditions of production leads psychoanalytic thinking to enclose itself in a misapprehension that is nothing short of ideological.

(a) Within psychoanalytic societies: Formation and transmission

Reflection on the way the practico-theoretical psychoanalytic corpus is produced, particularly the way in which training is conducted and transmission is secured, is neither gratuitous nor neutral. It is just such reflection that has set off movements that have strongly shaken the psychoanalytic world over the past fifteen years, especially in France. We have to emphasise that psychoanalysts are often ill-equipped to tackle these problems. It is not easy to reflect psychoanalytically on problems that are closely intertwined with political or socio-ethical problems. Appeal is quickly made to what is specifically psychoanalytic and problems are often set aside on the ground of an illusory neutrality. At the most concrete level, however, the psychoanalyst cannot escape facing a certain number of questions.

If one agrees to train other psychoanalysts, to transmit psychoanalysis, what are the links of autonomy and dependence between these psychoanalysts and their training analyst, between themselves and between these analysts and their successors? If the psychoanalyst refuses to take on the role of training others once he has become an analyst himself, what becomes of his autonomy in relation to those who trained him and to his future in relation to the perpetuation of psychoanalytic practice? Nobody can escape these problems, however marginal or independent he is. The analysis of these problems within analytic societies is sometimes easy enough to make, since the transference phenomena that are unacknowledged as such and that cause insoluble conflicts and massive identifications are obvious enough (to the observer). Indeed it is not easy to see how any human group can escape the play of these transferences, as S. Freud was the first to bring out in *Group Psychology and the Analysis of the Ego.*[1]

At the same time, even if it is easy enough for an alert psychoanalyst to unmask the transference phenomena that occur within his own analytic group, it is much more difficult for him to distance himself when the functions he himself fills within the group are in question, especially when these functions are hierarchised in such a way that a certain level of social responsibility automatically carries with it responsibility for training and transmission. Any critical evaluation of the ways in which this training and transmission are carried out will be irresistibly experienced as a questioning of the power exercised and will be rejected, not explicitly (of course!) in the name of this power but in the name of the integrity of the psychoanalytic cause. I have myself concretely lived through this situation quite enough to be able to state that the critical examination of the relationships of dependency within psychoanalytic societies has scarcely begun.

(b) Within societies of psychoanalysis: Autonomy of international relations?

When one is aware of the number of psychoanalytic societies in France, one cannot help asking about their autonomy in relation to each other and especially in relation to the *International Psychoanalytic Association* (IPA), founded by S. Freud himself in 1910.[2] The first French break with the IPA, brought about by J. Lacan in 1953, has created a situation in France which, far from being damaging to psychoanalysis, enriches and diversifies it, whatever one may have to say about any particular way of practising psychoanalysis or about any particular theoretical hegemony.

In this connection, since the ethics of liberation plays so important a part in this issue, I think it essential to report a little incident which will say much more than any long disquisition about the way in which the political autonomy of a movement that aspires to be international can be breached. Here I follow J. Derrida.[3] Number 144 of the Bulletin of the IPA makes mention of a request from the Australian Society of Psychoanalysis that the IPA make a pronouncement about the violations of human rights in Argentina. After numerous discussions and deliberations, the executive council of the IPA proposed a resolution that was carried in open vote by 85 per cent of those present. The resolution condemned attacks on liberty, the political use of psychotherapeutic treatment, etc., but it opened as follows: 'Along with numerous other international organisations the IPA has been informed of the violation of the rights of man perpetrated in *certain quarters of the globe*' (the italics are my own).

As R. Major says,[4] to the extent that the IPA refuses to specify Argentina, how can one avoid 'examining what *specification* means in the context of psychoanalysis. . . . The psychoanalytic community or institution, psychoanalysis itself, the very name of psychoanalysis cannot help facing this question sooner or later, on pain of being wiped out in its turn, and as soon as groups or institutions of psychoanalysts exist they clearly become implicated, in one way or another, with the forces that violate human rights, actively or passively colluding with them, in implicit or organised conflict.' We have to add, even if only to state the obvious, that a psychoanalysis based on confidentiality and professional secrecy cannot be practised when one of the actors in the therapy risks having the confidences made to him wrung out of him by violence. This amounts to saying that psychoanalytic autonomy is inexorably tied into a minimum guarantee of human rights.

(c) Autonomy in relation to the socio-economic-political context

Even in 'liberal' societies (which are not equally liberal for all the members who make them up) the practice of psychoanalysis is not independent of the socio-economic conditions which enable it to be carried on. Without wishing to enter into the question of 'élitism' or the enumeration of the conditions under which psychoanalytic therapy can begin (conditions connected with the place: hospital, consultation centres, private rooms—or with the person of the analyst: medically or not medically qualified, affiliated or not affiliated to a society of psychoanalysts) one thing at least is clear: money plays a part in the unfolding of the therapy, whether the analyst is directly paid or not, and whatever the method of payment. Any reflection on autonomy in the therapy or the autonomy of the therapy must at least take into account the connection with money and what that implies in the way of a relationship to the social and economic order, even if this reflection does not exempt the analyst from having to pronounce on the symbolic significance of the exchange or of the present. Similarly the autonomy of psychoanalytic practice in relation to the public authorities which could have jurisdiction over it (the tax, public health, scientific research and education authorities) must rest on a reflection on the nature of the scientific status of psychoanalysis that is not yet out of its infancy.[5]

2. WHAT IS THE PLACE OF AUTONOMY IN THE PSYCHOANALYTIC SITUATION?

As I have just indicated, the autonomy of the practice of psychoanalysis comes up against numerous obstacles, obstacles that lie within the societies of psychoanalysis themselves or that are tied to the inter-relationship of psychoanalytic societies amongst themselves, or obstacles that are due to the socio-economic conditions enabling the psychoanalytic situation to come about—or preventing it, as the case may be. So, within this psychoanalytic situation (bearing in mind that in the psychoanalytic realm the distinction between inside and outside is often not relevant) what is the status of the concept of autonomy?

(a) The initiating request

A desire for autonomy, for liberation, often features explicitly in the initial request that brings the therapeutic enterprise into being, as I suggested at the beginning of this article. Such and such a man racked by intolerable symptoms, such and such a woman prey to a depression that brings her time and again to the very edge of suicide, such and such a man or woman still subject to a stifling parental stranglehold, put this suffering in the foreground and wish to be delivered, freed from it. Many people also state that they do not feel themselves to be 'free' and would like to win their autonomy (whether sexual, professional, familial, social, political) in so far as they feel that they are not 'their own person' but seem to be driven by somebody else's desire, a desire that is all the more implacable for drawing its potency from being unconscious.

It goes without saying that these explicit demands represent only a minor part in the fundamental unconscious demand which is at work in the analytic enterprise. What needs to be added is that these desires to win autonomy are for the most part wished dictated by the intensity of the suffering experienced or by the depth of the malaise of feeling out of joint with one's own self-image or the image reflected back by others. The image that is sometimes given of psychoanalytic therapy as consisting in indulgence in the pleasant pastime of being soft on oneself or as an open sesame to all manner of licence, as the abolition of every constraint or social rule—this is a pure fiction. It is current to the extent that it feeds individual or collective resistance to analysis.

(b) The basic rule—the transference

Once the co-ordinates of the psychoanalytic situation have been established, what happens to these desires to become autonomous, to be liberated?

It is well known that the only 'basic' rule imposed on the patient (whether it is stated explicitly or arises in response to some anxious inquiry from the patient) is to say anything that comes to mind during the session, however banal, futile, insulting, gross this thought. To all appearances, then, there is a situation of total liberty, the only constraint on the analyst being to listen in a non-investigatory, non interrogative sort of way, in a 'free-floating' manner and with as much benevolent neutrality as possible. Now the rules of any game are an invitation to be bent, even to be broken, but the rules of the analytic situation are essentially inoperable.

For it is impossible to say everything—whether it is a case of insurmountable impediments of anguish, fear, shame existing to prevent one saying right out what one feels deep down or whether it is a case of the resistance to saying what comes to mind being so strong that it stops a conscious thought from even forming, something that expresses itself in an embarrassment about speaking, a sentiment of emptiness of thought, a 'I haven't got anything to say, I've got nothing in my head', always accompanied by a painful feeling. As for the psychoanalyst, free-floating attention and benevolent neutrality are at most goals never attained except asymptotically. What is more, the deep study of what goes on on the analyst's side, what some psychoanalysts call the counter-transference, tends to bring to light the analyst's affects and their connection with his infantile history rather than to evacuate all affect and thus transform—ideally?—the analyst into an impassible robot.

However the patient's reactions express themselves, they will unfailingly be transferred on to the person of the analyst. For a long time S. Freud thought of the transference as an obstacle to therapy, a foreign body in the pure seam of the unconscious. Gradually he came to recognise that the transference can indeed become an obstacle to the prosecution of the therapy but that more often than not it is its very engine, constituting the raw material thanks to which the psychoanalytic work takes place. There are two sorts of elements in the transference. Some, as the name indicates, derive from the roots in infancy or from the recent history of the patient: the psychoanalyst represents by turn (and whatever his or her real sex) this or that paternal or maternal, masculine or feminine, loved or hated figure (or all of these in the condensation of imagos or in the ambivalence of affects). But the transference also consists in the establishment between the patient and his analyst of a new, a present relationship. If this did not happen, it would be impossible to see how the analytic situation could escape from being a pure repetition of previous relationships, and as such death-dealing and insurmountable.

The prosecution of the therapy involves a series of modifications of the transference, modifications that ideally culminate in the patient taking his destiny into his hands, the destiny of which he feels he is and wants to be the subject: what happens to him is no longer the fault of his parents or of his analyst, but he questions himself about the unconscious desires that led him to this situation and, if he cannot master it, he wants in any case to make it his own business to manage. All this does not prevent the patient from feeling entirely dependent on the judgment of the analyst over most of the therapy, submitting himself to this judgment, even forestalling it by repeated declarations of guilt. This raises the extremely difficult problem of psychic determinism and chance. This is a general philosophical problem but it is desirable that psychoanalytic thinking makes its implicit expectations explicit to itself. In any case, once the axes of the therapy have been established, neither the patient nor the psychoanalyst can escape from the transference, all they can do is to bring it to light in the form of resistance to the transference, avoidance of the transference etc., which are so many analysable indices of a process of transference at work.

(c) Unawareness of the unconscious—A major form of alienation

It is clear that the analytic situation is not the only one to produce a transference or transference phenomena. We have already noted how they can be at work in psychoanalytic societies. What sets the transference in the analytic situation apart is that, far from being endured and tolerated as an inevitable accident, it is, along with other manifestations of the unconscious like dreams, slips of the tongue, mislaying things, one of the royal roads of the analysis of the derivatives of the unconscious. Even if one has to say with J. Haberman, as D. Mieth quotes him, that autonomy is 'the true identity of the moral subject, that is to say the true suppression of his alienation',[6] we still have to agree on what sort of status psychoanalytic anthropology as it has emerged from its practice reserves to the subject. The unavoidable constraint of the transference and the patient and progressive deliverance from it are not dangerous alienations created by the practice of psychoanalysis. What analysis amounts to is a particularly careful taking into account of and assumption of responsibility for what is at work in every human being. In other words, alienation consists not only in having neurotic symptoms and the consequences thereof but in awareness of the unconscious. Quite apart from any pathology, every human being is moved by unconscious impulses rooted in the unknown of his infantile prehistory.

In this perspective, the worst alienation is not to suffer from the constraint and mutilations of pathological phenomena which at least have the merit of being recognised as such, but to deny that the most lucid and alert reflective consciousness represents only the tip of the iceberg of the psychic apparatus immersed in the unconscious. Looked at from the point of view of the avatars of the transference, the psychoanalytic experience can hardly, at least over most of its duration, be considered to be an experience of becoming autonomous. Its detractors do not fail to rely on certain cases of interminable analysis in order to stigmatise it as an experience of alienation.

(d) So what can one expect of psychoanalysis in the way of autonomy?

So what can we expect of psychoanalysis? If the psychoanalyst agrees to undertake to work therapeutically with a patient, it is clearly because he implicitly believes that this will be for the good of this patient (as well as in the interests of the continuing pursuit of his own analysis), even if he can give the latter no assurance about the amount or the quality of the benefit involved. The question is whether this benefit can be described in terms of gaining or losing autonomy. It is very difficult to reply to this question, especially as the only person in a position to make a judgment about the analytic process initiated during the formal sessions and the consequences of this process is the patient himself. Some patients undertake an analysis for the sole purpose of freeing themselves from a situation which they feel and judge to be alienating but do not dare to undo. There are often cases in which the analysis undoes a bolt about to burst but in which once the result is achieved, the analysis then stops short.

The psychoanalyst is often asked about the possible *loss* involved in therapy: the loss of religious and family ideals, the loss of emotional investment in political, militant, sporting, intellectual pursuits. The question requires two sorts of response. On the one hand, it expresses the fear of exposing oneself in the course of the therapy to the anguish of losing an attribute meant to protect one from annihilation, abandonment: a fear that is symbolically called the fear of castration and which emerges in the course of every therapy in one form or another. On the other hand, this question goes back to the premonition the patient has about the nature of his ideals and his investment. To the extent that the investment is strongly tied to unconscious guilt-feelings to which the individual is subject and against which he struggles in making this investment, the lessening of guilt-feelings will probably go hand in hand with a lowering of the investment made. But we should not forget that the psychic energy locked up in the appeasement of guilt-feelings and of unconscious parental prohibitions etc. can, once freed, be reinvested in other domains of psychic activity. There can even be a reinvestment in the same domains but with a suppleness that is more fruitful than defensive rigidity.

It is not my business as a psychoanalyst to make a moral judgment about the use patients can make of the new forces liberated by analysis.

I am, however, convinced that it is not by means of fear, moral rigidity and unawareness of unconscious impulses (love and hate mixed up together) that one is going to promote the possibilities of liberation and solidarity contained in each human being.

Translated by Iain McGonagle

Notes

1. S. Freud *Group Psychology and the Analysis of the Ego*, S.E. XVIII pp. 67–143.

2. The following book about the history of psychoanalysis in France repays reading: E. Roudinesco *La Bataille de cent ans* I: *1885–1930* (Paris 1982).

3. J. Derrida in *Geopsychanalyse (Les souterains de l'institution)* Rencontre franco-latino-américaine (Paris 1981) pp. 16–17. The movement 'Confrontation', open to all tendencies in psychoanalysis but able to assume political responsibilities, devoted its issue No. 5, under the editorship of René Major, to the theme *Americo-Latina* (Paris 1981).

4. R. Major, in his intervention to the Franco-Italian colloquy *Psychanalyse et etat* (due for publication in 1983, in Milan).

5. The Collège de Psychanalystes, founded in Paris on 3 November 1980, which brings together psychoanalysts of different outlooks, intends to consider these questions and 'to study the repercussions of social pressures on the theory and practice of psychoanalysis, and, where necessary, to take steps calculated to ensure the integrity of the practice of psychoanalysis faced with the necessities or constraints involved in their being part of society' (extract from a by-law).

6. D. Mieth 'Autonomie. Emploi du terme en moral chrétienne fondamentale' in *Autonomie, Dimensions éthiques de la liberté* (Fribourg and Paris 1978) pp. 85–103 (citing Habermas at p. 96).

Marciano Vidal

Is Morality based on Autonomy compatible with the Ethics of Liberation?

The need for dialogue between 'autonomy' and 'Liberation'

WHAT I am trying to do in the following pages is to initiate a dialogue between morality based on *God-orientated autonomy*[1] and the ethical understanding derived from the Latin-American theology of Liberation. In the sub-title, the partners in the dialogue are identified in ethical/theological terms as 'autonomy' (understood as *God-orientated autonomy*) and 'Liberation' (understood as the source from which the *ethics of Liberation* are derived).

I cherish the hope and the belief that over the next few years the dialogue will prove to be a fruitful one. I also suspect that this task, though it can only be accomplished with the collaboration of all, will have to be the special concern of theologians in those language-areas which are clearly destined to be a bridge between two worlds. One such linguistic and cultural area is undoubtedly the Hispanic one.

I want to begin the dialogue, then, from two angles: (1) gathering together the objections of Liberation theology to morality based on God-orientated autonomy; and (2) giving expression to the warnings implicitly made from the standpoint of autonomy against any ethical pattern derived from Liberation theology. The outcome of the dialogue will be a brief conclusion in which I shall suggest a pattern of theological ethics which overcomes the difficulties of the two sides by bringing together the valid claims of both: a pattern of moral theology which may be defined as the *ethics of corporate emancipation*.

1. CRITIQUE OF 'AUTONOMY' FROM THE STANDPOINT OF 'LIBERATION'

What Liberation theology questions in the morality of God-orientated autonomy is the way in which it understands human responsibility in terms of *autonomy*. Liberation theologians are suspicious of the endorsement given to a particular socio-historical reality which is characteristic of the bourgeois and colonialist Western world. I shall first consider these suspicions and objections under the healing of 'Criticism of the bourgeois Enlightenment', then note the implications for the morality of autonomy.

(a) Criticism of the bourgeois Enlightenment

Autonomy is the mark and the ideal of the Enlightenment. Recent moral theology has tried to respond, albeit somewhat tardily, to the challenge of our enlightened modern age,[2] which seems to have set itself up as the incorruptible judge of the reasonableness of theological/moral discussion. The greatest and best reaction of theological ethics to the challenge of the modern age is to be seen in its acceptance of Kant's philosophy of practical reason. Kant has had a very decisive influence on theological ethics. The critical demand of Kantian autonomy is the pillar on which theological ethics tries to lean.

And yet it is precisely the Western Enlightenment which finds itself called into question from several directions by socio-historical criticism.

Among Catholic theologians, Metz is the one who has very courageously made the most pointed criticisms of the Enlightenment and its influence on religion (bourgeois religion).[3] For its part, Liberation theology too is alive to the present questioning of the Enlightenment, not only because of the type of person it has produced, but also, and especially, because the 'dream of reason has produced monsters', among which must be reckoned—in addition to wars, holocausts and social injustice—the economic and political colonialism pursued by the capitalist middle-class.[4] In consequence, Liberation theology demands that theological reflection should no longer be done by the same people, and that there should be a radical change of direction in the formation of Christian culture.

The ethics of autonomy still operate within the framework of the Enlightenment, and for that reason are open to the objections which have been mentioned. It has to be said of this kind of moral theology that it has not taken account of criticisms recently made of the socio-historical concepts of the Enlightenment. It is imperative, then, that it should change direction and change its spokesmen. Such a decision would re-orientate theological/moral reflection towards new geographical areas (the Third World) and towards human areas of Christian priority (the marginalised and the oppressed).

(b) Negative implications for the morality of autonomy

Once we have criticised the very essence of the morality of autonomy, on the grounds that it sprang from the bourgeois Enlightenment, it is easy to assemble objections to it. I shall simply list the main ones:

(i) The ethics of autonomy have legitimised and supported *bourgeois morality*, handmaid of the middle classes, and faithful ally of economic, social and political liberalism. It is clear that the 'virtues' of bourgeois morality cannot be the ultimate ideal for Liberation theologians.[5]

(ii) Ethical teaching which makes use of the socio-anthropological category of autonomy as its main hermeneutic principle, encourages a kind of *moral judgment* whose subject is the individual, whose channel is the optimism, the self-sufficiency and the arrogance of Promethean reason, and whose aim is progress achieved through a competitiveness which is insensitive to the situation of the weak, and which does not weigh the human cost on the path of development. The ethics of autonomy run the risk of becoming a *principle of disunity*; the hypertrophy of the autonomous subject leads to a *closed mind*, which has great difficulty in opening itself to the transcendence of human solidarity, and, in consequence, to the Transcendence of Grace. In questioning this model of judgmental morality, Liberation theology emphasises: God's freely-offered Promise as the origin of the moral imperative (the ethics of grace); human solidarity as the goal and the way (the ethics of solidarity); the need for a bias towards the weak (the ethics of the poor); and the community as the subject of liberation (the ethics of the people). The self-sufficiency and the lack of solidarity to be found in 'autonomy' result in an individualistic, private, falsely personal, élitist and idealistic morality, tied to the power of science, culture, economics, etc. 'Liberation' offers as an alternative a morality based on solidarity, especially with the poor.

(*iii*) Because of their connection with enlightened reason, the ethics of autonomy give priority to the reflective aspect, at the *expense of the narrative* aspect. Narration, however, is linked with the 'moral memory' of the people, and this memory clearly has a revolutionary and liberating role. To neglect the narrative aspect of ethics is to stifle the liberating voice of the people. It is not for nothing that Liberation theology proposes to restore the true moral heritage of the people by reading history 'in reverse', starting, that is to say, with those who do not figure in official history, with those beaten down by the power of injustice.

(*iv*) My final point concerns a feature which I regard as very negative and which I have written about elsewhere.[6] The ethics of autonomy have sought an *excessive conformity* to the modern world. This choice has caused them to *lose the messianic spirit*. Only the fresh air coming from Liberation theology can help theological ethics to recover their essential messianic role.

2. THE INTELLECTUAL WEAKNESS OF THE 'ETHICS OF LIBERATION'

I have tried to pay proper attention to the ethical output of Liberation theology, because I believe that it is likely to be one of the most productive sources for theological/moral reflection in the future. In various places I have expressed my views on the development of 'Liberation ethics'.[7]

As part of the present attempt at confrontation between 'the ethics of God-orientated autonomy' and 'the ethics of Liberation' I want now to suggest the main criticisms which can be made of the latter, in all intellectual honesty, from the standpoint of the former.

(a) The poverty of theological/moral reflection

The first point to notice is the *lack of studies* on the relationship between the world of ethics and Liberation theology. In setting itself up as reflection starting from and directed towards the praxis of liberation, Liberation theology appears to have a strongly accentuated moral dimension. If its deep theological originality consists in 'accepting the praxis (of liberation) as the source, the end and the criterion of the validity of theological theory',[8] then it is obvious that Liberation theology possesses *a nativitate sua* a constant ethical character. This new methodological approach has its historical origin in a set of factors which also direct reflection along ethical channels. The 'passionate' awareness of the unjust dependence of social groups or of whole peoples; the joyful acceptance of the Gospel of Liberation as an eschatological promise to be fulfilled in this world; the organisation of the people as themselves the bearers of their own destiny to be free; the choice of practical and theoretical measures for attaining a completely new orientation: all these are so many more signs of the ethical dynamism within Liberation theology. Its ethical quality cannot be denied.

In view of the strongly moral character of the basic theological stance, the lack of studies directly related to the subject of ethics stands out as all the more remarkable. There are some ethical allusions in the treatment of christological or ecclesiological themes; the documents of Medellín and Puebla contain ethical passages; ethical references can be found in the exposition and appraisal of the life of Christian communities (especially of so-called 'basic communities'); there has even been an attempt to tackle the problem as a whole and produce an interdisciplinary encounter on 'Christian praxis and ethical reflection in Latin-America'.[9]

Nevertheless it remains true that there is little in the way of real evidence. There does not exist any explicit, critical and systematic reflection on the assumed but never formulated 'ethics of Liberation'. The ethical allusions amount to no more than simple expressions of dissatisfaction, or fragmentary reflections. They do not imply any solid or consistent content. In a recent, well-considered assessment, which takes account of European political theology, it is recognised that 'obviously none of its representatives has yet produced a systematic treatment of ethics'.[10]

The absence of ethical reflection within Liberation theology had a valid explanation a few years ago. There were legitimate reasons for such silence: the desire to reject the conservative effect of traditional Catholic morality; the need to defend Liberation theology against those who wanted to reduce it to a mere reformulation of Catholic morality; the acceptance, at first uncritical, of the Marxist methodology, which is more concerned with the scientific analysis of the laws of the socio-historical process than with ethical formulations.

These reasons have now lost their force, and the lack of ethical reflection has thereby become more striking. In these circumstances there is clear need for a reformulation of theological ethics. I believe that the reason why this has not happened is that there are certain obstacles, inherent in the methodology of theology, which prevent genuine theological/moral reflection. I shall now try to show what these are.

(b) The confused epistemological status of theological ethics

The main difficulty with the 'ethics of Liberation' concerns their status as precise and independent knowledge. I am not referring to the epistemological status of Liberation theology in general, for this certainly cannot be said to be lacking in critical capacity. But, from an epistemological point of view, theological ethics, while they possess the characteristics common to all theology, have peculiarities of their own. It is to these that I am referring.

The particular role of theological ethics has been usurped by Liberation theology as a whole. On the one hand this has resulted in excessive 'confusion' between ethics and theology, and on the other it has hindered the 'diversification' of theological/moral knowledge within the general framework of theology. No one wishes to return to the false dichotomy between Dogmatic Theology (theoretical aspects of the faith) and Moral Theology (practical aspects of the faith). But we must not fail to recognise the special role of theological/moral thinking within the overall unity of the theological spectrum. Theological ethics use a more 'theandric' methodology than any of the other theological disciplines, since by definition they are concerned with both the practical reality of moral reasoning ('ethics') and the specifically Christian reference ('theological').

The usurpation of the ethical role by Liberation theology as a whole has resulted in a failure to distinguish, in theological/moral discussion, between the two distinct, though inseparable, aspects of theological ethics: (1) independent ethical reasoning (which, in precise language, is called 'categorial', and which forms the hermeneutical channel for the establishment of ethical standards); and (2) specifically theological reasoning (which, in similar terms, is called 'transcendental', and which establishes Christian concepts and their axiological application). Without this distinction it is impossible to determine the epistemological status of theological ethics.

In consequence of this lack of epistemological clarification, the ethics drawn from Liberation theology fall into a whole mass of ambiguities. Liberation theologians themselves have drawn attention to them: (1) the autonomy of intramundane moral reasoning is not fully recognised nor followed to its logical conclusion; (2) there is a strong tendency to reduce faith to its ethical demand, or at any rate to expand the 'demanding' side of belief, at the expense of its character as offer and celebration; (3) there is a risk of giving a religious sanction to worldly decisions, a sanction which leads to the 'sacralisation' of Left-wing politics.

Although there is no lack of recent studies on the epistemology of Liberation theology,[11] I still believe that the 'ethics of Liberation' will not attain their proper epistemological status as theological ethics so long as they do not recover their own proper role, and so long as they fail to distinguish between 'religious symbols with ethical content' (Kingdom, Hope, Promise, etc.) and 'intramundane ethical reasoning' (the autonomy, secularity and pluralism of historical factors).

The European/North American model of 'the ethics of God-orientated autonomy' should be an indication to 'Liberation ethics' of the need to distinguish and harmonise the *theological context* (religious concepts which express their moral content by means of 'ethical symbols'), and *independent reasoning* (practical intramundane standards of a secular, pluralist character).

(c) The framework yet to be constructed

The Christian communities which provide abundant examples of ethical commitment have, by comparison, produced remarkably little in the way of 'Liberation ethics' in written form. On the strength of such written ethical formulations as there are, and leaving on one side ethics actually lived out in the communities, it may be said that, basically, the content of Liberation ethics may be summed up as the affirmation of the *criterion of Christian orthopraxis*.

In Liberation theology praxis is the touchstone by which Christian coherence is tested. But what authenticates praxis? The answer to that question may be formulated in this way: what gives authenticity to Christian praxis is its *liberating character*. If we then go on to enquire what is the basis for this answer, we shall be told that that is the *promise*, that is the *Gospel*, that is what *believing in Jesus of Nazareth*, crucified and risen, means.

The criterion of orthopraxis is expressed in terms of a set of categories which, theologically, are very obscure. Such categories constitute the *clichés of Christian orthopraxis*. Here are some of them: 'The absolute criterion for ethics is "liberate the poor and the oppressed" '.[12] 'The basic criterion for ethical judgment is the human life of the real, concrete man'.[13] Knowing God means practising justice, and finds concrete expression in the praxis of love for the 'other', for the 'non-person', for the 'stranger'.[14]

After these categories of orthopraxis, we come down to the enumeration and analysis of a series of *values* (with the attitudes which correspond to them), the role of which is to form a bridge between the general criterion of orthopraxis and concrete reality. Those most commonly listed are of a dialectic character, and point to the following axiological contrasts: life-death; happiness-suffering; liberty-slavery; liberation-exploitation; identity-dependence; etc. It is not often that these values are examined in the concrete study of a moral topic. At the same time I do not know of any systematic analyses (as opposed to mere approximations) dealing with moral areas or topics in accordance with the methodology of the orthopraxis of Liberation.

We should not be too critical of the content of 'Liberation ethics' as it has just been described, since this is no more than a brief sketch based solely upon written evidence. In general terms it could well be said of Liberation ethics: that they make greater use of the rhetorical and paraenetical approach than of critical and scientific formulation; that they are expressed more in narrative descriptions than in reasoned arguments; that their music (language, concepts, categories, symbols) is notably monotonous and has a tendency to tedious repetition.

I believe that these judgments would be less negative if they were not the result of what I mentioned earlier in this article: the lack of any clear indication of the epistemological status of Liberation ethics. Because there is no precise distinction between the 'Christian context' and 'autonomous reasoning', the criteria of Christian orthopraxis operate within the faith itself. They do not have the validation of ethical reasoning; they are in large measure tautologous statements, based on dogmatic *a priori* arguments.

Liberation ethics are so heavily charged with religious content that practically everything in them belongs to the world of the 'transcendental', and far too little to the world of the 'categorial'. Orthopraxis is determined by religious symbolism. It leaves ethical reasoning with little room for action.

In this sense it can be said that the framework of Liberation ethics has yet to be constructed. By this I mean a *reflective basis* for the ethical system derived from Liberation theology. In this work of construction, there are, in my view, three priority areas:

(*i*) The establishment of an appropriate *foundation* for ethics on the basis of the presuppositions of Liberation theology. To achieve this two things need to be done: (α) The distinction must be established between eschatology and ethics, between promise and historical reality, between 'indicative' and 'imperative'. The ethical obligation of the believer is founded on the tension between these contrasting principles. (β) The orthopraxis of the faith must be publicly and rationally validated. This means entering into dialogue with intramundane thought, and using a less dogmatic and more interdisciplinary kind of language.

(*ii*) The *standard procedures* of theological ethics are unknown territory to Liberation ethics. It is necessary therefore to reconsider, in the light of the Gospel, and taking into account modern philosophy: (α) the structure of Christian moral judgment; (β) the meaning and the role of ethical standards; (γ) the interplay of different forces (individual-community; general-particular; etc.) in the development of ethical judgment.

(*iii*) Following on from these beginnings, the *actual content* of morality ought to be reconsidered, taking into account: (α) the need to widen the angle of vision so as to take in all the problems of human existence (and not to succumb to the temptation to tedious and monotonous repetition); (β) the need to discover and present historically valid and viable ways in which Christian values may be embodied (historical models of family, marriage partnership, personal relations, etc.); (γ) the need to offer an alternative model of Justice, over against existing models (contractual, libertarian, collectivist, etc.).

If the foregoing description is accurate, Liberation ethics are demands to be met rather than a verifiable guide to morality. In spite of that they should not be ignored or underestimated. They contain, in germ, all the criteria of Christian orthopraxis. They also carry with them an enormous potential of ethical/religious symbols, capable of bringing new vitality to our jaded theological/moral thinking. The need now is to set to work to construct a framework for theological ethics in accordance with the presuppositions of Liberation theology.

CONCLUSION

In this article I have noted, with a fair degree of emphasis, the criticisms made of each other by the ethical systems derived respectively from 'autonomy' and 'Liberation'. I need hardly add that these criticisms are also my own. Nevertheless I continue to take a positive view of both the *ethics of God-orientated autonomy* and the *ethics of Liberation*. Autonomy is of the essence of humanity, and is therefore the indispensable premise of ethics. Liberation forms the ethical/religious horizon of Christian existence.

A dialectical synthesis of the two approaches is possible. The morality of autonomy can retain its emancipatory force, provided that it carries out the methodological inversion required in changing its privileged spokesmen. The morality of Liberation will be able to go on offering the ethical ideal of the *active solidarity* of the Promise, provided that it respects the extent of the autonomy of secular reality.

The two emphases in question mesh together within the structural and functional unity of a new model of morality. Autonomy provides the 'text' of intramundane reasoning; Liberation offers the 'context' of the eschatological Promise. Autonomy becomes a process of emancipation; Liberation brings in the selective criterion of solidarity. In this way a new model of theological ethics comes to birth. They are the *Ethics of corporate emancipation*.

Translated by G. W. S. Knowles

Notes

1. On the meaning and justification of this pattern of morality (over against that of the 'ethics of faith'), see M. Vidal *Moral de Actitudes. I. Moral Fundamental* (Madrid 1981) pp. 196–227.
2. Various authors *Modernidad y ética cristiana* (Madrid 1981).
3. J. B. Metz *Faith in History and Society* (London 1980); *The Emergent Church: The Future of Christianity in a Post-Bourgeois World* (New York 1981).
4. G. Gutiérrez *La fuerza historica de los pobres. Selección de trabajos* (Lima 1979) pp. 303–394.
5. F. Ferrero 'La moral burguesa. Notas para su identificación y análisis' in *Moralia* 1 (1979) 205–216.
6. 'La preferencia por el pobre, criterio de moral' in *Studia Moralia* 20 (1982) 297–304.
7. ' "Teología de la Liberación" y ética social cristiana' in *Studia Moralia* 15 (1977) 207–218; *Moral de Actitudes. III. Moral Social* (Madrid 1979) pp. 127–136; 'La preferencia por el pobre, criterio de moral' in *Studia Moralia* 20 (1982) 277–304.
8. J. Lois 'Liberación (teología de)' in *Diccionario enciclopédico de Teología moral* (Madrid 1978) p. 1396.
9. The bibliographical references for the statements made in the text are to be found in the works mentioned in note 7. See also *Moralia* 4 (1982) 1–2: 'América Latina, problema moral'.
10. D. Sturm 'Praxis and Promise: On the Ethics of Political Theology' in *Ethics* 92 (1982) 733–750 (the passage quoted is from p. 733).
11. C. Boff *Teología de lo político. Sus mediaciones* (Salamanca 1980).
12. E. Dussel 'One Ethic and Many Moralities?' in *Concilium* 150 (1982) 54.
13. P. Richard 'La ética como espiritualidad liberadora en la realidad eclesial de América Latina' in *Moralia* 4 (1982) p. 109.
14. G. Gutiérrez, the work cited in note 4, *passim*.

Dietmar Mieth

Autonomy or Liberation:
Two Paradigms of Christian Ethics?

1. THEOLOGY'S REACTION TO AUTONOMY

THE CONCEPT of autonomy is central to the Enlightenment, in which the thought of Immanuel Kant has a determining role. This suggests that the way theology sees autonomy is connected with Enlightenment ideas in theology. Initially the relationship between theological ethics and Kant's idea of autonomy was a negative one. An exception to this is the theologian Sebastian Mutschelle (1749–1800), who tried to integrate Kantian ethics into theology. Mutschelle formulates the moral principle in close connection with Kant's categorical imperative: 'I ought always to will and to do only that which evinces respect for every rational being, for each and every human being, for myself and others, honouring each according to his intrinsic worth, as an end in himself, neither regarding nor using anyone as a means for some other end'.[1] This formula clearly reveals the theologian's interest in the Kantian idea of autonomy. He is interested in the fact that human dignity is beyond manipulation, is an end in itself. This human dignity is expressed by the term 'rationality', i.e., that which is specific to the human being. Thus the universality of reason becomes an ethical criterion. According to the model of autonomy, therefore, ethics is grounded in reason. Its implications are expressed in universal respect for human dignity. Hence, as a theologian, Mutschelle is particularly interested in the Enlightenment's human rights ethos. This does not mean that theology has no role in ethics. Theology's task is to interpret the laws of morality. Reason is receptive to theological interpretation, indeed it needs it, because, as the precondition of man's humanity, it must ultimately be referred to God. God is 'the ground of existence of that rationality which binds me'.[2]

Besides providing a deeper interpretation of reason, theology must take seriously the revelation of ethical reason found in the teaching of Jesus. This teaching, of course, is never supra-rational. It does not contain supplementary instructions. But the teaching of Jesus does provide a greater moral certainty in matters of reason. Finally, theology has the task of motivating and activating the ethical reason and ethical action.

In thus welcoming ethical autonomy, Sebastian Mutschelle is in danger of seeing theology primarily as natural theology, and ultimately as human ethics. To prevent theology from degenerating into religion, and the Christian ethos of faith from becoming a rational ethical code, most nineteenth century German theologians saw that it was appropriate to set up a revelation ethics as a foil to the ethics of the Enlightenment. In this view, Christian ethics has a specific foundation of its own.

The more the so-called 'secularisation of morality' proceeded step by step with the history of middle-class society, the more Christian ethics was obliged to reconsider the idea of an autonomous ethical basis in human reason. Surprisingly enough the idea of autonomy crops up in the documents of the Second Vatican Council, mainly in *Gaudium et Spes*. What we find here and in the document *Dignitatis humanae*[3] is not, in fact, ethical autonomy, but there is stress on the autonomy of created reality. This idea of autonomy, of the intrinsic validity of creation, is meant to be the key to a new dimension of openness to the world. Putting it in a rather over-simplified form, the Pastoral Constitution is basically underlaying the idea of autonomy with St Thomas Aquinas' notion of autonomy. French theologians like M. D. Chenu had no qualms about applying the idea of autonomy to the interpretation of natural morality in Scholasticism. Thus the concept of autonomy invokes the tradition of natural morality. True, the Thomist definition of ethical conduct, '*secundum rationem agere*' rests on an explicit theology of creation and an explicit anthropology, but all the same it does stress the practical reason as the source of ethical judgment. This practical reason is given to all men. That is why Thomas Aquinas too can say that the New Law contains no new ethical commands over and above the prescriptions of the natural law.[4]

Certainly there is a difference between Thomas Aquinas and Immanuel Kant or his disciples. According to Thomist teaching the reason cannot provide an ultimate foundation for ethical conduct. Rather, it is the method by which moral *judgments* are arrived at. So it is not by chance that the Second Vatican Council recognises autonomy in the sense of the intrinsic value of earthly reality, but does not directly recognise ethical autonomy.

Theologians like Alfons Auer have carried this process further.[5] Their prime concern is to show that, in locating the basis of the ethical reason in God, we need not find ourselves in opposition to the Kantian view, particularly if we do not confuse theology with the teaching of religion, which according to Kant should take place within the limits of pure reason. If we start from the idea that God is a postulate of the practical reason, theology— even though its God is not a postulate but the real God of revelation—will not see ethical autonomy as being in conflict with the ultimate basis of ethical conduct in God. For human reason's practical autonomy, which has already been affirmed in the tradition of natural morality, simply refers to the way by which ethical insight takes place. It does not mean that man's ethical reason can be held to be 'independent' of God. Autonomy does not imply autarchy. Kant himself drew a definite distinction between human autonomy and divine autarchy. The man who is pledged to his own human dignity can by no means do whatever he likes. In the Kantian sense, such arbitrary action is the hallmark of heteronomy. Thus it was possible to observe a convergence between philosophical ethics in Kant's sense and the basis for moral reason as established by theology. This is a view which has had a great influence in German moral theology in the last decade. The model of 'autonomous morality within a Christian context' became widely normative in Christian ethics, an approach which promoted an interest in human rights in theology. Of course, the acceptance of the idea of autonomy by no means meant that Kant's formal ethics had been adopted. We have already seen that Mutschelle's interest in Kant's ethics and categorical imperative related to the material, rather than the formal aspect. Whether Kant can be interpreted in this way is still a matter of dispute. But an interpretation of this kind does bring the categorical imperative closer to the person-based approach of Christian social teaching.

Although self-evident in Christian social teaching, the person-based approach led to conflict, signally in the area of birth control. Here the personal criteria seemed to contradict the universal structure of human nature. This is why the conflict between moral theology and the Church's teaching office, on the relationship between personal and natural morality, is still going on.

However, we are not concerned with the discussion about concrete ethical norms. At least as far as theory is concerned, the dialogue between theology and autonomy on the status of the ethical reason seems to have yielded some clarity. Now we are facing the objection (from both philosophy and theology) that the 'autonomous' approach in ethics is too individualistic. True, moral judgment can be generalised and argued, and these operations are universal criteria of the individual human reason, but we cannot automatically assume the presence of transcendental reason and freedom in the empirical individual. The notion of autonomy seems to take too little account of the factors which limit concrete freedom, i.e., the 'world's sin', sin in the social structures and in the life of the individual. Observations such as these recall Hegel's criticism of Kant's moral philosophy and the criticisms applied by the theologies of 'orthopraxis' (political theology, liberation theology) to the individualism and 'imperialism' of European middle-class Enlightenment. Reflection on the transcendental conditions of freedom does not, according to this critique, automatically produce freedom in the concrete. Freedom is a process subject to historical and social influence, and this means that reason's *de facto* freedom cannot be taken as an ethical standard. Here we are faced with a fundamental opposition between transcendental philosophy and historical dialectic. The notion of autonomy is seen as too 'optimistic' in its assumption of positive rationality in given reality, whereas in fact this reality is the arena of man's oppression, irrationality and heteronomy. Man is not emancipated by reflection but only by a historical and active process of liberation, a process which must first prepare the way for man's concrete freedom and for his openness to universal reason.

2. THE CONCEPT OF LIBERATION IN THEOLOGY AND ETHICS[6]

Autonomy is also a liberation concept, though it is understood primarily as liberation through reason. But if reason is seen historically as a mere tool, as a false rationalism, as simply reflecting the history of human oppression, it cannot be the starting point for the history of man's freedom. In such a case it only exemplifies the negative side of the historical process. Theology tries to respond to this insight by emphasising practical *experience*, in opposition to Kant and in continuity with Thomas Aquinas, as the locus of reason. Furthermore, if we attain ethical insight through experiencing 'contrasts', the appropriate starting point for ethics seems to be liberation rather than transcendental freedom. This occurs in practical terms where people strive for concrete liberation as a result of their particular experience of its opposite, e.g., in the history of the emancipation of women and in the liberation of the peoples of the Third World, which is only just beginning. An important insight gained from the practical process of liberation is that individual freedom is not possible except on the basis of solidarity in liberation. Thus ethics becomes dependent on liberation in action. In a manner of speaking, moral reason arises out of the praxis of liberation.

Here the individual aspect of personal values is moved from the centre of interest in favour of the dialogue aspect and in favour of the dialectical view of history. The starting point is not autonomy but the idea of a solidary and communicative freedom. Human reason is subject to the historical process; it too needs to be attained as a result of a process of liberation.

Reflections such as these are already backed up by theology. The history of the ethos of the people of God in Israel and in the primitive Christian communities can without difficulty be seen as the gospel of progressive liberation. This liberation is eminently a theological process, a process of God's saving acts. But this theological process meets with a contrary theological factor in history, for history also exhibits evil. It can be seen as the failure to liberate, expressed in concrete unfreedom (imprisonment, exile). Therefore a theology of liberation is inconceivable without a theology of sin. Sin arises out of man's urge to dominate, where his ('autarchic') assertion of his own freedom implies oppression of the other, something which cannot be reversed by individual conversion of life. Corresponding to this theology of collective liberation ('people's theology'), therefore, there must be a practical ethos of liberation, an ethos of the people of God. This is why, in the perspective of liberation, the importance of basing moral judgments on human reason is replaced by the importance of the practical ethos. In Hegel's sense, ethos is more important than morality. But if this practical ethos is discovered in the liberating praxis of Christians, it owes its existence to God's liberating praxis as recognised by faith. The experience of contrasts which yields Christian ethos is determined by the faith of Christians in God's liberation.

So reflection about praxis is replaced by reflection arising out of praxis. This means, for instance, that it is very hard to draw up general solutions to problems in advance, before they have been worked on practically. On the one hand, we are striving for concrete utopias; on the other, we are concerned only about the steps immediately ahead of us. This provides a better basis for an ethos of change than by trying to shape praxis according to predetermined ethical judgments. From the point of view of theological ethics, what we have is diagnosis rather than integration. Whereas autonomous ethics in a Christian context is heavily dependent on analytical reason, striving to analyse scientifically the various experiences, here we have an analysis of faith, which shows 'reasonable' solutions to be in fact subservient to extrinsic interests. Thus, in the analysis of faith, the promotion of birth control at the discretion of the individual in Third World countries would, in the light of the contrast of the Third World suggested by faith, be seen as an instance of the centre oppressing the periphery.

The liberation-ethos approach has affected particular aspects of the Christian faith. It has resulted in the re-thinking of soteriology, for instance, from the point of view of man's total liberation. It has affected the connection between christology and ethical praxis.[7] Whereas, at the Enlightenment, the danger was that Christ was seen primarily as the ethical Teacher, and the 'rational' Jesus absorbed the Christ of faith, now Jesus' own praxis of liberation is not regarded christologically, as setting a pattern: it is interpreted in terms of soteriology. Christ the liberator means that the incarnational process has not come to an end; it passes over into the eschatological process: history is seen as the decision in favour of the full incarnation, hominisation, of man. Sacramental theology, too, becomes part of the eschatological diagnosis of reality and a sign of this decision.

The ethics, or rather, ethos of liberation thus begins with a fundamental existential act of conversion. But this act does not refer only to the isolated individual. Rather, it signifies entry into a new solidarity, and is characterised by the 'option for the poor'. If a person is to belong to Jesus Christ in the sacramental sign of salvation, offered to him as the gift and opportunity of new life, he must take part in this act of solidary conversion which gives him a place in the new people of God, he must *be* Church, so to speak, for his fellow men. Conversion in solidarity yields the ethos of the people of God, which is manifested in its diagnosis of social reality, in the new integration it imparts to the community, in a new coherence of theory and praxis, action and contemplation. The ethos of liberation unfolds like this: first there is the diagnosis reached by faith's analysis, then comes the inspiration which grows out of common contemplation, liturgy, and incipient political action; fundamentally, each step can be superseded by the next, so that human life can be continually transformed and made more human. This is why liberation ethos rejects the universal system of a certain kind of ethical thought. Here ethics is decentralised, as is reason too. Those who champion universal reason always make it an instrument of domination on the part of the centre. To say this is not to deny the usefulness of reason in expressing and applying the diagnosis of faith. But it is not reason which justifies faith: faith itself yields its own reason, and this alone can really liberate man in the full sense.

The Christian ethics of liberation has no alternative, then, but to be a political ethics. All the factors which condition the process of man's liberation are political in kind. This presupposes, of course, that State and society cannot be seen as separate. Autonomous ethics and liberation ethics must have different ideas as to what is 'political'. For autonomous ethics is always in danger of dissociating the political from the personal. It sees politics as a matter for the politician's autonomous reason. In liberation ethics political responsibility cannot be other than shared. The danger here is that the individual is pushed to the fringe of solidary, political action.

My main concern is not to weigh up the dangers and opportunities of autonomous ethics in a Christian context as compared with Christian liberation ethics, but to show that both approaches are paradigms of Christian ethics, and that, to the extent that they are Christian, i.e., aware of their dependence on faith if they are to come to maturity, they need not be in conflict. In my view they could together embark upon a learning process. First I should like to outline this common learning process and then indicate the restructuring it would bring about in the ethical priorities of 'autonomous ethics in a Christian context'.

3. A COMMON LEARNING PROCESS

A common learning process needs a common basis. The ability to experience freedom and act ethically is supplied by the trust and hope which are elicited in the community of faith. Many approaches must be rejected on account of their negative consequences: the Enlightenment brand of optimism, the evolutionary belief in progress, confidence in an automatic historical dialectic. We now know the price paid for middle-class liberalism in the Third World; we are aware of the limitations of expansion, the totalitarian results of class struggles. The idea of complete liberation can only be entertained in an eschatological context. Without trust in the liberation which God will bring, a man has either to believe in a historical fruition or to act in pure protest against man's destruction, not seeing any evidence of success. In the first case he puts his trust in a utopian deliverance which leaves out of account all those who have suffered in the past and are still suffering now. In the second case he is without hope, yet cannot associate himself with the general indifferences of the uncompassionate society.

Autonomous ethics and liberation ethics are both anchored in a faith without which there could be no hope of the recognition of ethical obligation. They differ only in their emphasis. The ethos of autonomy is a personal, human rights ethos, and as such cooperates, beyond faith, with all men of good will. It is concerned not only to reveal the indispensable rational basis of ethical conduct, but also to promote man's liberation in the concrete, so that he can live under the rule of law and, on this basis, act ethically. The ethos of liberation is an ethos of solidarity with the oppressed, seeking the shortest way to concrete liberation, so that man himself can be transformed. There is reciprocal influence of the individual on society and of society on the individual.

The one has confidence in human nature and in ethical reason (see for instance the history of Catholic social teaching—with all its shortcomings—which exemplifies autonomous ethics in a Christian context), and the other puts its trust in the fact of God's prior liberating acts, seeing his continued action in the solidarity of the people which cleaves to him. These two approaches share a liberating hope in the face of an uncertain future; they are also one in the active awareness of the dangers which are evidently connected with this future.

To be successful, a common learning process presupposes not only a common basis but also differences which resist easy reconciliation. These can be traced to ineradicable differences in the way history is experienced. In its insistence on the communicable ethical reason common to quite different men, and in its consistent devotion to the rational explication of ethical judgments, the ethos of autonomy is ultimately responding to a basic insight, namely the insight into the danger of the human ethos becoming overgrown with rank religion, as was manifested in the European wars of religion. This is why the ethos of autonomy is suspicious of a *direct* connection between the diagnosis of sin which springs from the experience of contrasts generated by faith on the one hand, and practical social action on the other. It insists that the criterion of ethical reason should mediate between faith's impulse and concrete action. Of course this criterion can be misapplied in the ineluctable interplay of understanding and personal interest, but this does not disqualify it.

By contrast, the liberation ethos insists that ethical insight is determined by one's practical standpoint. No one can act ethically unless he is already working practically for liberation in solidarity with others. If a man does not share the inspiration of ethical insight, of practical reason, which only comes through common action, his judgment will lack the conviction of personal involvement. He is reflecting on praxis from the outside, not from within. He is laying claim to an apparent, but spurious neutrality in ethical judgments.

It seems to me that we are here dealing with different perspectives of a single hermeneutical process, operating between the poles of liberating ethics and liberating praxis. They illustrate the primal unity-in-tension between a praxis which leads to reflection upon itself, and a theory which is empty unless it produces practical results. The two will be able to collaborate if, within this tension, each perspective cultivates what is proper to it.

4. IN THE COMMON LEARNING PROCESS WITH THE CHRISTIAN LIBERATION ETHOS, THE CHRISTIAN ETHICS OF AUTONOMY MUST CHANGE ITS PRIORITIES

We observed that the ethics of autonomy is concerned to provide a basis for ethical judgments in the universality of reason. This endeavour is supported by the human rights ethos, which (like all particular interests) leads to understanding. From a Christian point of view this ethos is grounded in man's acceptance and liberation by God.

The Christian liberation ethos teaches us to distinguish between the middle-class version of the human rights ethos, which continually comes up with new 'rights', new ideas of what is necessary for individual happiness, personal relationships and social recognition, and a new human rights ethos according to which the first step towards justice is the equal right to life, and to life under the rule of law. The middle-class version implies the recognition of a proliferating diversity of individual needs, the demand for a higher quality of life, and the overcoming of personal suffering. Here are three examples: in the advanced medical technology whereby an externally fertilised embryo is implanted into the womb, people speak of the 'right' to have one's own child. Then, in the context of abortion, the World Health Organization once referred to the child's 'right' to be 'wanted'. Thirdly, in 1977 the Human Rights Commission of the Council of Europe declared it to be a human right that no one should have to undergo 'unreasonable' suffering. Now obviously it is a good thing for a mother to have a child of her own, for children to be wanted, and for pain to be combated. But we must ask whether these 'rights' are not in fact only available to the few—put bluntly, whether they are really privileges of the rich. Surely we ought to be able to accept other children as well as our own? Should we not hold the damaged life of the unwanted child to be as valuable as any other? Ought we not to learn to appreciate the universal proportions of suffering before making the individual case into a paradigm? The ethos of liberation does not simply deny the possibility of greater or lesser nuances in the liberation of the individual, but where action is concerned its priorities must be different. The problems often put forward in the ethos of autonomy become small indeed when compared with the weight of suffering endured by the many who lack even the right to life.

'There is no such thing as other people's suffering' (Konstantin Simonov).[8] If the poor are not liberated, if their liberation continues to be obstructed by the 'liberated' middle-class, there will be more and more psychic damage inflicted on the indifferent and uncompassionate individuals who seek to cultivate their own petty freedoms. This can be seen in the rising suicide figures, in aggression and self-destruction, in the inability to live humanely in faithfulness, warmth and tenderness. The ethos of liberation teaches us that, in seeking our own liberation, we must go beyond ourselves. There is no such thing as other people's suffering, and this applies to other people's liberation too. In accepting responsibility for others we are also furthering our own growth. Faced with the pain of our own self-destruction, we become aware that it is a precipitation, in our own soul, of the pain of others. The demand for greater and greater differentiation in the expression of personal freedom (N.B. not the legitimate need for individual freedom itself) destroys liberation, for it takes no account of the cost of this greater differentiation. By turning our hearts and minds to bring fullness of life to those without rights, we are taking a step forward in the realisation of our own liberation, at the very centre of freedom, not at its periphery.

Once we have become aware of this, we must change the priorities of autonomous ethics, and of the human rights ethos too. In doing so we must not sacrifice the claims of reason. We must adhere to a strict methodology. But instead of devoting attention to borderline questions of individual freedom, we ought to take up the issues of survival itself: the question of survival in an environment fit for human life; the question of the quality of a life subject to bureaucratic and technological systems; the question of fair distribution in the face of growth-limits and shortages; and finally the question of peace and thus of the disarmament campaigns. If it adopts these priorities, the ethics of autonomy too will have the fresh quality of an interest in liberation that generates new understanding.

Translated by Graham Harrison

Notes

1. S. Mutschelle *Moraltheologie oder theologische Moral, Erster Teil, Allgemeine Moral* (Munich 1801) p. 67; quoted in A. Auer *Autonome Moral und christlicher Glaube* (Düsseldorf 1971) p. 133.

2. The work cited in note 1, at p. 100.

3. Also in the *Decree on the Apostolate of the Laity*, no. 7.

4. See for instance *Summa Theologiae* 1a. 2ae q. 107,4. And see A. Auer, the work cited in note 1, at p. 129.

5. See note 1. See also the documentation presented by A. Bondolfi in this issue.

6. See the Latin-American contributions to the present issue.

7. See J. Sobrino *Christologis desde america latina* (Mexico ²1977).

8. See on this and what follows: D. Sölle 'Mystik und Widerstand' in *Neue Wege* 77 (1983) 283–293.

PART IV

Documentation

Alberto Bondolfi

'Autonomy' and 'Autonomous Morality': Research in Progress round a Key-Word

THE PURPOSE of this article is to provide bibliographical documentation on a debate that has arisen within the German-speaking theological world since the second half of the seventies, to indicate how the other countries of the 'First World' have reacted to it, and finally, to give some indication of how it might be linked with the new theology of the 'Third World'.

1. ALFONS AUER'S THEME AND ITS SEQUEL

Unlike other basic theological subjects, Auer's proposal of 'an autonomous morality in a Christian context' was originally taken up and discussed only in German Catholic theology. In 1971, Alfons Auer, already fairly well known as a theologian for his work on the theme of *Gaudium et Spes* and similar subjects,[1] published his *Autonome Moral und christlicher Glaube*,[2] which attracted a lot of attention, but without provoking, at least for some time, any notable adverse criticism.[3]

Auer speaks of autonomous morality in a sense close enough to that used by the second Vatican Council in its pastoral constitution on the Church in the Modern World,[4] as a 'yes to reality', an assent made by the Christian seeking to live by the light of his faith. Wordly reality is, by etymological definition,[5] dynamic, sensible and good even in its mutability and radical historicity.

Any work seeking to lay down ethically valid norms should take account of this vision of reality. This, according to Auer, needs to be done in successive stages: in the first place, any research in this field will refer, whether consciously or not, to a 'pre-understanding'[6] of what the world is. The establishment of norms itself will then be done in three distinct stages, defined as 'rooting in social sciences', 'anthropological integration' and 'normative intervention of ethics'.[7] Both in *Autonome Morale* . . . and his subsequent works,[8] up to 1981, Auer does not seem to make any effort to give a precise semantic definition of what he means by the term 'autonomy'.[9] The autonomy of ethics he defends seems to originate in the tradition of thinking about natural law: in the first place the various types of knowledge belonging to the natural sciences are autonomous, as are various degrees of learning, and so is ethical reflection in relation to dogmatic theology.

If one looks for greater terminological exactitude, it must be recognised that at the end of the sixties Auer did not have recourse to lexicographical reconstructions such as would satisfy a moralist seeking to use the complex locution 'autonomy' in a differentiated fashion.[10] His latest works witness to his recognition of the need to take account of the 'history of the effects' (*Wirkungsgeschichte*) of this term. I will try here to document some stages in the historical reconstruction of autonomy, giving preference to those works that spring most directly from the theological debate occasioned by Auer's proposition. He himself refers back to the Enlightenment moralist S. Mutschelle (1749–1800)[11] in order to show that not all Catholic moralists reacted negatively to Kantian thought.

In the same line of thinking, Auer, who sees no contradiction between Kantianism in morality and the Christian moral message, examines his concepts through the history of both philosophy[12] and theology.[13] He recognises that there is still much to be done to uncover the prejudices and commonplaces affecting relations between the Enlightenment and Christian ethical thought.

Auer generally supports the balance of argumentation in favour of the autonomous character of theological ethics in the thought of Thomas Aquinas.[14] He is not alone in defending this conviction, but has been accompanied and followed by a series of scholars who have tried to document this interpretation in their inquiries into the different works of the great medieval theologian.[15] But, as we know, the term 'autonomy' is not found in the works of the Angelic Doctor, and this leads to a suspicion that the use of the term in Auer and other German theologians stems from a locution that does not exist in other languages but has come to be translated in them as 'autonomy': the word *Eigengesetzlichkeit*.[16]

The ambiguity attaching to the fact that, outside the German language, the word 'autonomy' can be referred indiscriminately to the human person, to moral reflection, or to different sectors of social life, has provoked a fair number of difficulties in understanding Auer's propositions and their expression in other German-speaking theologians.[17]

The philosophical historical investigation of the same subject has not been particularly detailed or abundant, though its critical utilisation has helped the debate between moral theologians to gain something in clarity.[18] What has been lacking above all is detailed critical study of Kant's view of the autonomy of the will by the Frankfurt school, and a taking-up of this point in the theological field.[19]

2. A 'GERMAN' AND 'CATHOLIC' DISCUSSION

From the mid-seventies there has been much discussion in Germany of Auer's position and that of other moralists working on the same wavelength. The chief voice in this debate (which cannot be reconstructed here for reasons of space) has been that of B. Stöckle, professor of theological ethics at the University of Freiburg im Breisgau.[20] The word 'autonomy' he considers theologically inopportune, if not illegitimate, on both historical[21] and systematic grounds.

This line of thought places most emphasis on the theonomous and christological nature of the ethical norms of the New Testament, and the ethically productive role of the ecclesial community.[22] In the second half of the seventies, the terms of the debate became an object of concern to some organs of the Catholic ecclesial *magisterium*, such as the German bishops' conference and the international theological commission. While the first body did not get around to defining its position publicly, the second did express itself indirectly through its organisation of two colloquies on the subject.[23]

3. EUROPEAN AND INTERCONFESSIONAL WIDENING OF THE DEBATE

It would be a misrepresentation at this point to suggest that the range of opinions on the proposition that ethics can be autonomous in a Christian context is limited to those simply in favour and those against. The key-word 'autonomy' is used in moral theology in other contexts and with other meanings.

Some Polish moral theologians, for example, inspired by the ethical methodology deriving from Anglo-Saxon analytical philosophy, propose an 'autonomous' ethic in the methodological sense with respect to dogma on the one hand and the empirical sciences on the other.[24] Such views and concerns are less evident in the theological ethics of the German, Italian and English-speaking worlds,[25] and completely lacking in the French.[26] The varying degrees of interest with which this basically German debate has been followed in the Mediterranean countries has led some scholars to attempt the first systematic studies of the whole question of 'autonomy'.[27] These syntheses show that the whole debate has, at least till now, remained an excessively 'intra-Catholic' affair.

If the proposition had been taken up to any significant degree by the theologies of the various Reformed traditions, this would surely have taken the discussion into new areas. The internal debate in Catholic moral theology has been followed with some interest in Evangelical quarters,[28] though not to the extent that one can talk of a real parallel debate going on.[29]

4. WHAT NEXT?

Over a decade of discussions among Catholic moralists has not led to a final clarification of the question: Who and/or what is autonomous with respect to whom and/or what? Here one can ask whether a clarificatory contribution to this somewhat tired debate could and should come from the theology of the Third World. Personally, I would rather leave the question open, limiting myself merely to observing that perhaps the way to greater clarity might be found through critical analysis of the contradictions inherent in the ideals of autonomy and of emancipation in the modern age.[30] The theologians of both hemispheres need to contribute their own socio-cultural insights into this general problem in a concerted effort. Within the plurality of emancipations and autonomies of history, the Redemption remains a unique fact for Christians.

Translated by Paul Burns

Notes

1. A. Auer *Christ sein im Beruf. Grundsätzliches und Gesichtliches zum christlichen Berufsethos* (Düsseldorf 1969); *id. Weltoffener Christ. Grundzätliches und Geschichtliches zur Laienfrömmigkeit* (Düsseldorf⁴ 1964).

2. *Id. Autonome Morale und christlicher Glaube* (Düsseldorf 1971).

3. The only exception known to me is that of the moralist G. Ermecke. See his review of *Autonome Morale . . .* in *Theologische Revue* 63 (1972) 138–142; *id.* 'Christlichkeit und Gesichtlichkeit der Moraltheologie' in *Catholica* 26 (1972) 193–211.

4. The concept of 'the autonomy of earthly affairs' in *Gaudium et Spes* n. 36, the 'rightful autonomy of the creature', and 'false autonomy' in n. 41, the 'autonomy of many areas of human life' in the *Decree on the Apostolate of the Laity* n. 1, and the 'autonomy of temporal things' in n. 7.

5. Auer plays on the word *Wirk-lichkeit* to show that reality is not perceived only as a brute fact, but as full of active potentiality. In this sense, *Wirklichkeit* translated Eckhart's term *actualitas*. See D. Mieth *Die Einheit von vita activa und vita contemplativa in den deutschen Predigten und Traktaten Meister Eckharts und bei J. Tauler* (Regensburg 1969), as well as *id.* 'Meister Eckharts Ethik und

Socialtheologie' in *Meister Eckhart heute* ed. W. Böhme (Karlsruhe 1980) pp. 42–57.

6. On this theme, see Auer 'Das Vorverständnis des Sittlichen und seine Bedeutung für eine theologische Ethik' in *Studia Moralia* 15 (1977) pp. 219–257.

7. Auer's original terms are 'humanwissenschaftliche Grundlegung, anthropologische Integrierung, ethische Normierung'.

8. See Auer 'Die aktualität der sittlichen Botschaft Jesu' in *Die Frage nach Jesus* ed. A. Paus (Graz 1973) pp. 271–363; *id.* 'Ein Modell theologische-ethischer Argumentation "Autonome Moral" ' in *Moralerziehung im Religionsunterricht* (Freiburg 1975) pp. 27–57; *id.* 'Die Bedeutung des Christlichen bei Normfindung' in *Normen in Konflikt* ed J. Sauer (Freiburg 1977) pp. 29–54; *id.* 'Autonome Moral und christlicher Glaube' in *Katechetische Blätter* 102 (1977) 60–76; *id.* 'Christianity's Dilemma: Freedom to be Autonomous or Freedom to Obey?' in *Concilium* 110 (1977) 47–55; *id.* 'Die Bedeutung der christlichen Botschaft für das Verständnis und Durchsetzung der Grundwerte' in *Werte-Rechte-Normen* ed. A. Paus (Graz 1979) pp. 244–259; *id. Ethische Normen. Das christliche Proprium* (Bensberg 1980); *id.* 'Absolutheit und Bedingtheit ethischer Normen' in *Unterwegs zur Einheit. Festschrift für H. Stirnimann* ed. I. Brantschen and P. Selvatico (Freiburg 1980) pp. 345–362; *id.* 'Zur Rezeption der Autonomie-Vorstellung durch die katholisch-theologische Ethik' in *Theol. Quart.* 161 (1981) 2–13.

9. This effort to define terms precisely is nevertheless central to Auer's contribution in *Theol. Quart.*, the article cited in note 8.

10. The first thing to note is how pre-Vatican II Catholic thought tended to interpret post-Kantian thinking as a series of variations on a single attitude summed-up under the heading 'autonomism'. Thus the *Lexikon für Theologie und Kirche* has no article on 'autonomy' but only a single column on 'Autonomismus': see LThK I, pp. 1131–1132; see also H. E. Hengstenberg *Autonomismus und Transzendenzphilosophie* (Heidelberg 1950); H. K. Kohlenberger 'autonomismus' in *Historisches Wörterbuch der Philosophie* I, pp. 788–792. Two lexicographical monographs, useful both for the use and reception of the terms, appeared only after the publication of Auer's work: K. Hilpert 'Autonomie' in *Wörterbuch der christlichen Ethik* (Freiburg 1975) pp. 28–34, supports the theological position that would refute any idea of autonomy in Christian ethics; for a careful study of Protestant theological thinking on the subject, see E. Amelung 'Autonomie' in *Theologische Realenzyklopedie*, V, pp. 4–17.

11. Auer *Autonome Moral* ... cited in note 2, pp. 131–136. For a study of this writer, see W. Hunsheidt 'Sebastian Mutschelle. Ein kantianischer Moraltheologe' in *Moralphilosoph und Moralpädoge* (Bonn 1948) and above all the monograph by Ch. Keller *Das Theologische in der Moraltheologie. Eine Untersuchung historischer Modelle aus der Zeit des deutschen Idealismus* (Göttingen 1976). In French there is a monograph from the early years of this century: G. Diebolt 'La Théologie morale Catholique en Allemagne au temps du Philosophisme et de la Restauration (1750–1850)' (Strasbourg 1926). As recent research into the whole period of the second half of the eighteenth century I know only of the extremely detailed study by M. Casula *L'Illuminismo critico. Contributo allo studio del'influsso del criticismo kantiano sul pensiero morale e religioso in Germania* (Milan 1967). Yet Casula's research has not been used either by Auer or by his critics: see *supra*, particularly the article by Hilpert. For an analysis of biblical motifs present indirectly in the philosophy of the German Enlightenment, see A. P. Kustermann 'Biblische Motive als Argumente in Autonomie-Denken der Aufklärung' in *Theol. Quart.* 161 (181) 33–42.

12. See M. Forschner *Gesetz und Freiheit. Zum Problem der Autonomie bei I. Kant* (Munich-Salzburg 1974). See also J. Schwartländer, 'Nicht nur Autonomie der Moral—sondern Moral der Autonomie' in *Anspruch der Wirklichkeit und christlicher Glaube* ed. D. Mieth and H. Weber (Düsseldorf 1980) pp. 75–94; *id.* 'Sittliche Autonomie als Idee der menschlichen Freiheit. Bemerkungen zum Prinzip der Autonomie im kritischen Idealismus Kants' in *Theol. Quart.* 161 (1981) 20–33. A piece of exegetically deep research recently undertaken is E. Feil 'Autonomie und Heteronomie nach Kant. Zur Klärung einer signifikanten Fehlinterpretation' in *Freiburger Zeit. für Phil. und Theol.* 29 (1982) 289–441, which in my view succeeds in definitely eliminating a whole series of misunderstandings of Kant's thought.

13. See an alternative appreciation in the thick volume by I. Mancini *Kant e la teologia* (Assisi 1975); see also R. Mokrosch and L. Wilkens 'Die Vernuft-und Geweissenautonomie bei Kant als Quelle des bürgerlichen Selbtsvertändnisses' in *Evang. Theol.* 20 (1973) 386–402, and B. Quelquejeu 'De deux formes autoritaire et autonome de la conscience morale' in *Revue des sciences phil. et. théol.* 65 (1981) 233–249. For a very detailed comparative study of the texts, see F. Compagnoni 'La Dignité de l'homme selon E. Kant et Vatican II' in *Autonomie. Dimensions éthiques de la liberté* ed J. Pinto de Oliveira (Fribourg-Paris 1978) pp. 124–142. See also the analytical study by J. Hoffmann 'Zur Kantrezeption innerhalb der Moraltheologie' in *Münchener Theol. Zeit.* 31 (1980) 81–109.

14. As early as *Autonome Moral*, Auer had devoted some pages to Thomas Aquinas, at pp. 127–131. Later, he elaborated his thoughts in his article 'Die Autonomie des Sittlichen nach Thomas von Aquin' in *Christlich Glauben und Handeln* ed. K. Demmer and B. Schüller (Düsseldorf 1977) pp. 31–54.

15. Two recent doctoral theses have taken up the subject, studying in detail the treatise 'De lege' from the *Summa theologica* and Aquinas' Commentary on the NT: see K. W. Merks *Theologische Grundlegung der sittlichen Autonomie* (Düsseldorf 1978) and B. Bujo *Moralautonomie und Normenfindung bei Thomas von Aquin unter Einbeziehung der neutestamentlichen Kommentare* (Paderborn 1979). For an interpretation bringing out more the theological nature of Thomas's morals and structured around the virtue of faith, see S. Pinkaers 'Autonomie et hétéronomie en morale selon S. Thomas d'Aquin' in *Autonomie. Dimensions éthiques de la liberté*, cited in note 13, pp. 104–123, esp. 109. *Id.* 'La Morale de S. Thomas est-elle chrétienne?' in *Nova et Vetera* 51 (1976) 93–107. Auer's interpretation is close to the conclusions reached by J.-M. Aubert 'La Specificité de la morale chrétienne selon Thomas' in *Le Supplément* 23 (1970), no. 92, 55–73, and also to those of J. de Finance 'Autonomie et Théonomie' in *Thomaso d'Aquino nel suo settimo centenario* (Rome 1974) pp. 239–260; D. Mongillo 'Poter normativo della "ratio" nella Legge Nuova' in *Angelicum* 51 (1974) 169–185; B. Montagne 'Autonomie et dignité de l'homme' in *ibid.*, 186–211.

16. The use of the term in Protestant theological ethics can be found from the end of the last century in the wake of works by E. Troeltsch and W. Hermann. When, in this sense, they talk of autonomy (*Eigengesetzlichkeit*) of various sectors of life, politics, economy, the arts, law, etc., they mean that these sectors need not necessarily refer to ordinances of a religious nature to order their affairs. This is not so much Kantian autonomy in action as an ideal of the organisation of knowledge stemming from Descartes. For a history and classification of the concept, see A. Hakamies 'Der Begriff "Eigengesetzlichkeit" in der heutigen Theologie und seine historischen Wurzeln' in *Studia Theologica* 24 (1970) 117–129; *id. Eigengesetzlichkeit der natürlichen Ordnungen als Grundproblem der neuer Lutherdeutung* (Witten 1971). For a more modern concern and particular attention to the Catholic position, see M. Honecker 'Das Problem der Eigengesetzlichkeit' in *ZfThK* 73 (1976) 94–130.

17. A larger number of German writers agree with and follow Auer's viewpoint. As a necessarily incomplete selection of recent studies, see F. Böckle 'Theonome Autonomie. Zur Aufgabenstellung einer fundamentalen Moraltheologie' in *Humanum*, ed. J. Gründel and V. Eid (Düsseldorf 1972) pp. 17–46; *id.* 'Theonomie und Autonomie der Vernunft' in *Fortschritt wohin?* ed. W. Oelmüller (Düsseldorf 1972) pp. 63–86; *id.* 'Der neuzeitliche Autonomieanspruch' in *Studia Moralia* 15 (1977) 57–77; J. Fuchs 'Autonome Moral und Glaubensethik' in *Ethik im Kontext des Glaubens* ed. D. Mieth and F. Compagnoni (Freiburg 1978) pp. 46–74; D. Mieth 'Autonome Moral im christlichen Kontext' in *Orientierung* 40 (1976) 31–34, a particularly informative article on the discussion occasioned by Auer's work. The same applies to the next article, useful for those who do not read German: D. Mieth 'Autonomie. Emploi du terme en morale chrétienne fondamentale' in *Autonomie. Dimensions éthiques de la liberté*, cited in note 13, pp. 85–103. The whole volume examines the semantic field of autonomy (together with other key words close to it, such as emancipation, responsibility, freedom, etc.) with a methodology fairly close to what is known in German as *Begriffsgeschichte*. In the same line, see S. Pfürtner 'Autonomie des Menschen—Autonomie Gottes' in *Begegnung* (Graz 1972) pp. 345–359; B. Schüller 'Sittliche Forderung und Erkenntnis Gottes. Ueberlegungen zu einer alten Kontroverse' in *Der menslische Mensch* ed. B. Schüller (Düsseldorf 1982) pp. 28–53; S. Piegsa

'Autonome Moral und Glaubensethik. Begründung der Autonomie aus dem Glauben' in *Münchener Theol. Zeit.* 29 (1978) 20–35; V. Eid 'Zum Verhältnis von Autonomie im christlichen Ethos' in *Theol. Quart.* 106 (1980) 191–203; and finally the profound synthesis provided by E. Schillebeeckx in 'Glaube und Moral' in *Ethik im Kontext,* cited above in this note, pp. 17–45.

18. See H. Czuma *Autonomie. Eine hypothetische Konstruktion praktischer Vernunft* (Munich-Freiburg 1974). With a much more pessimistic outlook on man's possibilities of achieving the ideal of autonomy, and following more the direction of Adorno's thought, see R. Zur Lippe *Bürglerliche Subjectivität. Autonomie als Selbstzerstörung* (Frankfurt 1975). A recent very succinct speculative research into our subject is provided by R. Bittner *Moralisches Gebot oder Autonomie* (Freiburg 1983); for knowledge of the more important philosophical texts, see M. E. Scribano *Morale e religione tra seicento e settecento* (Turin 1979) and P. Roubinet 'Hétéronomie et autonomie de l'homme du XVIIᵉᵐᵉ siècle' in *Rev. des sciences phil. et theol.* 64 (1980) 423–425.

19. This what O. Marquand set out to do in his article 'Idealismus und Theodizee' in *Schwierigkeiten mit der Geschichtphilosophie* (Frankfurt 1973) pp. 52–65. I have also essayed an analogous conception in A. Bondolfi *Teoria critica ed etica cristiana* (Bologna 1979).

20. See in particular B. Stöckle 'Autonome Moral. Kritische Befragung des Versuches zur Verselbständigung des Ethischen' in *Stimmen der Zeit* 98 (1973) 723–736; *id. Grenzen der autonomen Moral* (Munich 1974) pp. 723–735; *id.* 'Zum Ethos und der Ethik' in *Diskussion über H. Küngs "Christ sein"* (Mainz 1976) pp. 113–46; *id.* 'Normerkenntnis und Normbestreitung' *Normen in Konflikt* ed. J. Sauer (Freiburg 1977) pp. 9–28; *id.* 'Flucht in das Humane' in *Int. Kath. Zeit.-Communio* 6 (1977) 312–325; *id. Handeln aus dem Glauben. Moraltheologie konkret* (Freiburg 1977). In the *Wörterbuch der christlichen Ethik,* cited in note 10, Stöckle has written the article on *ethos,* while his collaborators K. Hilpert and H. Oberhem have done *Ethik* and *Methodologie* together, Hilpert alone contributing *Autonomie.*

21. See above all K. Hilpert 'Die theologische Ethik und der Autonomie-Anspruch' in *Münchener Theol. Zeit.* 28 (1977) 329–366, and his great historical enquiry *Ethik und Rationalität. Untersuchungen zum Autonomieproblem und zu seiner Bedeutung für die theologische Ethik* (Düsseldorf 1980). This inquiry stresses, rightly to my mind, the important part played in the history of the ideal of autonomy by the 'deformation' worked on Kant by Feuerbach and Nietzsche. This inquiry has given rise, by reason of its apologetic intent in confronting Stoöckle's thesis, to two particularly critical though illuminating reviews: F. Inciarte 'Theonomie, Autonomie und das Problem der politischen Macht' in *Theol. Rev.* 78 (1982) 89–102, and B. Schüller 'Eine autonome Moral, was ist das?' in *ibid.* 103–106.

22. See H. Schürmann 'Die Gemeinde des Neuen Bundes als Quellort des sittlichen Erkennens nach Paulus' in *Catholica* 26 (1972) 15–37; *id.* 'Die Frage nach der Verbindlichkeit der neutestamentlichen Wertungen und Weisungen' in *Prinzipen christlicher Moral* (Einsiedeln 1976) pp. 11–39. For a hermeneutical approach more favourable to an 'autonomously' based ethos, R. Hasenstab *Modelle paulinischer Ethik. Beiträge zu einem Autonomie-Modell aus paulinischer Geist* (Mainz 1972). W. Wolbert in *Ethische Argumentation und Paränese in I Kor. 7* (Düsseldorf 1981), shows himself attentive to the distinction between normative and incidental discourse.

23. See *Prinzipien christlicher Moral,* cited in note 22, in particular the following contributions: H. Urs von Baltasar 'Neuen Sätze zur christlichen Ethik' pp. 69–93; J. Ratzinger 'Kirchliches Lehramt-Glaube-Moral' pp. 43–66. See also the volume edited by W. Kerber *Sittlicher Normen. Zum Problem ihrer algemeinen und unwandelbaren Geltung* (Düsseldorf 1982).

24. See H. Juros 'Die "Objektschwäche" der Moraltheologie' in *Person im Kontext des Sittlichen* ed. J. Piegsa and H. Zeimentz (Düsseldorf 1979) pp. 13–21; T. Styczén 'Personaler Glaube im Spannungsfeld von religiöser Autorität und Gewissenautonomie' in *ibid.* pp. 30–68; *id.* 'Autonomie und christliche Ethik als methodologisches Problem' in *Theologie und Glaube* 66 (1976) pp. 211–219; *id.* 'Autonome Ethik mit einem christlichen "Proprium" als methodologisches Problem' in *Ethik im Kontext des Glaubens* cited in note 17, pp. 75–100.

25. Exceptions are the works by B. Schüller already cited, and the inquiries by W. Wolbert and S. Privitera: of the latter, see *L'uomo e la norma morale. I criteri di individuazione delle norme morali*

secondo i teologi moralisti di lingua tedesca (Bologna 1975); *id.* 'Per un interpretazione del dibattito su "l'autonomia morale" ' in *Rivista di teologia morale* 12 (1980) 565–585; *id.* 'Autonomia: istanza storica e riflessione etica' in A. Bondolfi *et al.*, *Autonomia ed emancipazione. Verso un nuovo rapporto tra fede e morale* (Turin 1982) pp. 39–96. In English, see *inter alia*, J. J. Walter 'The Dependence of Christian Morality on Faith: a critical Assessment' in *Eglise et Théologie* 12 (1981) pp. 237–277.

26. As far as the French language is concerned, it cannot really be said that there has been a debate, but rather simply a transmission of the elements of the debate. See R. Mengus "L'Universel et le germanique. Une enquête sur l'état de la morale dans les grandes Facultés de théologie catholique de la RFA' in *Recherches de science religieuse* 70 (1982) 109–130; A. Bondolfi, 'Autonomie ou théonomie: une alternative pour la morale chrétienne? Présentation et évaluation de débat en cours entre moralistes de langue allemande' in *ibid.* 161–180; R. Tremblay 'Par delà la "morale autonome" et "l'éthique de la foi", à la recherche d'une *via media*' in *Studia Moralia* 20 (1982, no. 2) 223–237. In Spanish, see particularly M. Vida 'La fundamentación de la ética teológica como respuesta al reto de la modernidad. Exposición crítica del estado de la cuestión' in *Moralia* 3 (1981, no. 11–12), 419–446; C. Diaz 'Etica libertaria y ética cristiana' in *ibid.* 403–418; E. B. Estébanez 'Autonomía del hombre y quehacer ético' in *ibid.* 389–402.

27. For an overall view of the semantic aspects of the question, see the collective volume issued by the Institute of Moral Theology at the University of Fribourg, ed. by J. Pinto de Oliveira, *Autonomie. Dimensions éthiques de la liberté*, cited in note 13; also S. Bastianel *Il carattere specifico de la morale cristiana. Una riflessione dal dibattito italiano* (Assisi 1975); *id. Autonomia morale del credente. Senso e motivazione di un'attuale tendenza teologica* (Brescia 1980); E. Chiavacci 'Il dibattito sull' autonomia della morale' in *id. Responsabilità e norma morale* (Bologna 1978); F. Citterio 'Morale autonoma e fede cristiana: il dibattito continua' in *Scuola Cattolica* 108 (1980) 506–561 and 109, 3–29; H. Oberhem 'Ethik und Glauben. Zur logischen Structur moral theologischer Normenbegründung' in *Münchener Theol. Zeit.* 31 (1980) 188–209. The most complete synthesis known to me is O. Bernasconi *Morale autonoma ed etica della fede* (Bologna 1981). This is a doctoral thesis presented at the Angelicum in Rome.

28. For an introduction to the position taken by Protestant theologians, see E. Amelung 'Autonomie', the article cited in note 10; H. Blumenberg 'Autonomie und Theonomie' in *Religion in Geschichte und Gegenwart*, I³ pp. 788–792; P. Tillich 'Theonomie' in *ibid.*, V² pp. 1128–1129; H. Thielicke *Mensch sein—Mensch werden* (Munich 1975). It is relatively rare to find modern Protestant theologians taking up positions directly related to Auer. Exceptions are: M. Honecker 'Technischer Sachzwang oder ethischer Autonomie' in *Evangelische Kommentare* 10 (1977) 592–594; *id.* 'Der Streit um die autonome Moral. Ein Katholischer Disput, der auch Protestanten angeht' in *Lutherische Monatschefte* 18 (1979) 151–154; W. Dantine 'Die konziliare Idee einer Dialektik von relativer Autonomie der irdischen Wirklichkeiten und heilsgeschichtlicher Dimension der Kirche. Eine Variante zu Luthers Weltverständnis?' in *Materialdienst des Konfessionskundlichen Instituts Bensheim* 28 (1977, no. 2), 25–29. A Catholic reaction to the doubts expressed in the Protestant camp about the proposition of an 'autonomous' theological ethic is D. Mieth ' "Natürliche" Theologie und autonome Ethik' in *Anspruch der Wirklichkeit und christlicher Glaube* (Düsseldorf 1980) pp. 58–74.

29. There is a certain number of parallels in the debate between G. Ebeling and W. Pannenberg on the subject of the crisis of ethics and its evidence: see G. Ebeling 'Die Evidenz des Ethischen und die Theologie' in *ZfThK* 57 (1960) 318–356; W. Pannenberg 'Die Krise des Ethischen und der Theologie' in *Theologische Literaturzeitung* 86 (1972) 7–16; G. Ebeling 'Die Krise des Ethischen und die Theologie' in *id. Wort und Glaube*, II, pp. 42–55; W. Pannenberg and G. Ebeling 'Ein Briefwechsel' in *ZfThK* 70 (1973) 448–473. On this debate, see J. Werbik *Die Aporetik des Ethischen und der christlicher Glaube. Studien zur Fundamentaltheologie G. Ebelings* (Munich 1976); H. Ringeling 'Emanzipation und ethische Gewissheit' in *id. Neue Humanität* (Gutersloh 1975) pp. 65–78. See a final contribution from Ebeling 'Zum Verhältnis von Dogmatik und Ethik' in *Zeit. für evangelische Ethik* 26 (1982) 10–18.

30. For a beginning of a possible confrontation between European and Latin American theologians on this subject, see the basic historical study by E. Dussel 'Periodizzazione di una storia

H

della chiesa in America latina' in *Cristianesimo nella storia*, 3 (1982) pp. 253–286; G. Ruggieri 'Nuovi soggetti alla ricerca della loro storia: una proposta latino-americana' in *ibid.* pp. 287–295; D. Mieth 'Autonomy of Ethics—Neutrality of the Gospel' in *Concilium* 155 (1982), pp. 32–39. On the contradictions inherent in the idea of emancipation, see A. Bondolfi 'Emancipazione: note di lessicografia e di ricezione teologica' in *Autonomia ed emancipazione*, cited in note 25, pp. 9–35; D. Zillessen 'Emanzipation' in *Theologische Realenzyklopedie* 9 pp. 544–552.

Mary Christine Morkovsky

Bibliography for Liberation Ethics

THEOLOGY OF liberation criticises the totality of the present world system, shuns dualisms and dichotomies, obtains theoretical insight in and through concrete and communal involvement or orthopraxis, identifies with the oppressed and poor, and works with them to upset oppressive structures so that the world will be more humane. Liberation ethics is not one branch of liberation theology but rather its pervasive theme. In this article I will identify only the main Latin American, Black, and feminist authors of the past dozen years whose ethical thinking reflects most clearly these five characteristics.

Gustavo Gutierrez has as his point of departure the human need for liberation from sin, passivity, and oppression in order to be in communion with God and neighbour, participate creatively in society, and make wise choices.[1] To become poor with Christ today is to be in solidarity with those who are struggling for their basic rights. The poor are products of a system that creates and justifies poverty. In the very process of constructing a different social order, God is encountered and utopia is verified in praxis.

Enrique Dussel's is the most developed liberation ethics to date.[2] He criticises ethics founded on values or ends and grounds ethics in openness and service to the other as other in order to construct a new and more just reality in the basic areas of economics, erotics, and politics. Ethics uses not only dialectic but *analectic* founded in faith in an other beyond the system of totality and on responsibility before the absolute other for the human other. The religious utopia of life face-to-face without domination is both the practical postulate of the ethics of any concrete historical project and the absolute ethical criterion with regard to its foundation.

Juan Luis Segundo says the distinguishing mark of a liberation theologian is the suspicion that all ideas are bound up with social situations.[3] To be faithful to Christian tradition he uses a *hermeneutic circle* and a dialectic that combines the criteria of social analysis and the sense of the collective consciousness with Scriptural tradition and God's purpose of redemption. Divine revelation does not give a total, absolute moral code unaffected by time; the moral code extracted from divine revelation varies according to humankind's maturity.

Leonardo Boff points out that the liberation of Christ and God is *more* than socio-political liberation, but it *is also* that. Work to transform history anticipates the liberation of God's Kingdom and also articulates, conceptualises, and facilitates the appearance of the unthinkable and ineffable origin of any process of liberation.

Hugo Assmann finds abstract or a-historical faith to be an insufficient criterion for ethical choice. In the Incarnation, God becomes other; in the historical embodiment of faith, the Christian empties self and loses self in the other. The way the oppressed others view the world is *epistemologically privileged* because their view is closer to reality than that of the rich. There is no separately existing sphere of truth distinct from the sphere of reality; the criteria governing ethical choice are to be liberated in practice by constant tests against experiments. The works of Severino Croatto, Segundo Galilea, Arturo Paoli, Jon Sobrino, Beatriz Melano Couch, María del Carmen Leñero, Anabella T. Yañez, Rubem Alves, Jose Miguez Bonino, and Sergio Arce Martinez are also along the lines of liberation ethics. Its themes may also be detected in songs from the '*Misa Popular*' of Guatemala and Nicaragua, in 'La Symphonie des Deux Mondes' authored by Dom Helder Camara, in testimonies repeated by Ernesto Cardenal and Arturo Paoli, or in Negro Spirituals.

The most developed Black liberation ethics[4] is that of James H. Cone. The ethical question of human doing is inseparable from what God is doing to free the oppressed. To find out what to do, one can use the Bible and experience. Scripture shows Jesus identified with outcasts not because he felt sorry for them but to reveal God's judgment on political and religious structures that oppress the weak. Faith helps one realise that the eternal structures of creation empower the oppressed and that transcendence granted in the resurrection gives an other-wordly dimension to freedom. Human beings are free only in the liberating encounter with the source of freedom, God who is present in but not limited to experience.

Cone sees fighting for civil rights in a capitalist system as insufficient. Society needs to be restructured along the lines of a creative socialism. One must decide whether to support the violence of the oppressors who control the present unjust order or the violence of the oppressed who participate in the present system against their will.

Other Black ethicians are less given to sharp distinctions than Cone. For J. Deotis Roberts ethics must begin with God's will manifested in the present, but eschatology is the basis of Black hope. Christian ethics is founded not in formal principles or agape but rather in whatever makes life human, liberates the oppressed, provides meaning and hope in suffering, and fosters unity. Christian ethics exceeds moral philosophy in demanding forgiveness and reconciliation, and violence is inconsistent with it.

Major J. Jones distinguishes between covenant and agape. Christian ethics makes love its intention, purpose, and norm. The Old Testament reveals that the chosen have serious obligations, and Jesus' actions were not conditioned by the actions of oppressors toward him. Nonviolence is preferable; however, if conditions are such that a Christian takes life, it would be more honest to admit that the action beyond this point is not Christian or ethical. Social justice is a divided question. It does not require the same of the socially advantaged white person as it does of the socially disadvantaged black person. The works of Joseph R. Washington, Jr., also have liberation as a unifying thread.

Radical feminist writers like Mary Daly[5] severely criticise traditional morality that extols selflessness, sacrificial love, and passive virtues. Her own message is a witness or call rather than an abstract theory. Jesus modelled a kind of contagious freedom, a pointing to potential for further liberation, and a call to affirm one's own unique being. She finds the real significance of the virginity of Mary in genuine feminine autonomy in the context of sexual, parental relationships. The Assumption signifies hope for the collective psyche's effort to overcome a rigid dichotomy between good and evil as well as sexual stereotyping.

The prolific historical theologian Rosemary Ruether frequently touches on issues in feminist ethics.[6] The ethics of competitiveness and technological mastery is tied to the image of God as male, creating out of nothing, transcending nature, and dominating history. True, women and other victims of oppression are not saints; their inner being is distorted, filled with self-contempt and tendencies to self-destruction and fratricide. Their sense of integral personhood will be recovered only by passing through the important stages of anger and pride. Among the tasks remaining if ethics is to reconcile people with the earth are a fundamental restructuring of the socioeconomic relationship between domestic support structures and work in which male roles of alienation and conflict shape values, and a fostering of reciprocal relations in which the self is actualised in the very same processes that support the autonomy and actualisation of others.

Letty M. Russell[7] insists that the method of feminist theology is inductive and seeks the right questions and hypotheses concurrent with praxis, which verifies thinking. In technological society, all parts of the globe are linked in impersonal structures of violence and injustice. Thus Christians are called to *macro-charity* for people caught in dehumanising structures; issues of technological exploitation, nation building, and global peace are urgent. We are also called to *proleptic mistakes* (for example, protests and demonstrations) which anticipate the future, create signs of hope, and contradict the problems themselves. The Christian vocation to partnership is to service and to *transeunce* which, unlike transcendence, emphasises the beyond *within* history. True partners understand that power is the possibility of self-affirmation rather than the means to control and destruction.

Elizabeth Schussler Fiorenza questions the theological model of biblical interpretation.[8] The process of interpreting Scripture is not necessarily liberating, and it is undeniable that the Bible has been used as a political weapon. Feminists find the Bible to be inherently sexist and thereby destructive of women's consciousness. Since every historical expression of the faith is ideological, it can be falsified and serve the oppressor. It is constantly necessary to ask whose existence and whose God is being interpreted. The criterion for appropriate interpretation can only be the personally and politically reflected experience of oppression and liberation. Janice Raymond underlines the importance of androgyny, originating in an intuition of being rather than in the Bible or in natural law. Valarie Goldstein Saiving contributes the valuable observation that the temptations of women *as women* are distinctive. They are not to pride or will to power but to underdevelopment or negation of the self, to excessive dependency, mistrust of reason, distractability, and diffuseness.

Most male liberation ethicians from North America are Protestants.[9] Robert McAfee Brown emphasises the need for conversion, for living 'life from below' in order to see reality. John C. Bennett reiterates that although God loves all, he is partial to the victims of society.

Frederick Herzog contributes a valuable interpretation of the fourth gospel. The starting point of liberation is God's solidarity with the oppressed and its implications for us. He urges his readers to 'think Black', to acknowledge their compassionate, corporate personhood rooted in unconcealment. If the self is corporate in the first place but appears separated when human beings abuse power, then transcending the self may not be the essence of morality. Peter C. Hodgson is sympathetic to liberation ethics but claims to be unidentified with any one specific liberation theology. J. Andrew Kirk grasps the view that a new eschatological order is subversive of existing structures, but his search for an *a priori* justification of reasons and methods for liberation is not characteristic of liberation ethics. Daniel L. Migliore, Henry Shue, John M. Swomley, and Lee Cormie also incorporate liberation views in their works.

Jürgen Moltmann and Johannes B. Metz are the Europeans acknowledged to be most influential in the early development of theologies of liberation, but they do not seem to trust that the risk of actual involvement will enable them to work out criteria. Denis Goulet actually does liberation ethics.[10] In all his works he tries to restore the link between morality and economic science. Gerard Fourez's ethics,[11] influenced by Bergson, is liberationist in flavour though he does discuss some individual relationships not directly related to social structures. Other European thinkers supportive of liberation ethics include Georges Casalis, Charles Duquoc, and Enda McDonagh.

Notes

1. *A Theology of Liberation* (Maryknoll 1973) (Teología de la Liberación, Salamanca 1974); *Liberation and Change* (Atlanta 1972).
2. *Filosofia etica Latinoamericana*, 5 vols. (México 1977, Bogotá 1979, 1980); *Ethics and the Theology of Liberation* (Maryknoll 1978).
3. *Liberation of Theology* (Maryknoll 1976). L. Boff *Teología del cautiverio y de la liberación* (Madrid 1978). H. Assmann *Theology for a Nomad Church* (Maryknoll 1976). J. S. Croatto *Exodus* (Maryknoll 1981). J. Miguez Bonino *Doing Theology in a Revolutionary Situation* (Philadelphia 1975).
4. *A Black Theology of Liberation* (New York 1970); *God of the Oppressed* (New York 1975). J. D. Roberts *Liberation and Reconciliation* (Philadelphia 1971). M. J. Jones *Christian Ethics for a Black Theology* (Nashville 1974).
5. *Beyond God the Father* (Boston 1973); *Gyn-Ecology* (Boston 1978).
6. *Liberation Theology* (New York 1972); *New Woman/New Earth* (New York 1975).
7. *Human Liberation in a Feminist Perspective* (Philadelphia 1974); *The Future of Partnership* (Philadelphia 1979).
8. *In The Challenge of Liberation Theology*, ed. B. Mahan and L. D. Richesin (Maryknoll 1981).
9. R. M. Brown *Theology in a New Key* (Philadelphia 1978). J. C. Bennett *The Radical Imperative* (Philadelphia 1975). F. Herzog *Liberation Theology* (New York 1972); *Justice Church* (Maryknoll 1980). P. Hodgson *New Birth of Freedom* (Philadelphia 1976). J. A. Kirk *Liberation Theology* (Atlanta 1979). D. L. Migliore *Called to Freedom* (Philadelphia 1980).
10. *The Cruel Choice* (New York 1973); *A New Moral Order* (Maryknoll 1974).
11. *Liberation Ethics* (Philadelphia 1982) (Choix ethiques et conditionnement social, Paris 1979).

Contributors

ALBERTO BONDOLFI was born in Switzerland in 1946, and studied philosophy and theology at the University of Fribourg, where he lectured from 1971 to 1977. Since 1979 he has taught at the Institute of Social Ethics at the University of Zurich. His published works include *Teoria critica e etica cristiana* (1979), and he has contributed articles to the *Rivista di teologia morale*, *Recerches de science religieuse*, *Social Compass*, *Orientierung* and other journals. He is President of the Swiss society of religious sociology.

ENRIQUE DUSSEL was born in Argentina in 1934. He holds doctorates in philosophy from Madrid and in history from the Sorbonne, and an honorary doctorate in theology from the university of Fribourg. Dr Dussel is professor of ethics in the Autonomous National University of Mexico and professor of the history of theology and the history of the Latin American Church at the Mexican Theological Institute for Advanced Studies. He is also president of the Commission for the Study of the History of the Church in Latin America (CEHILA). His publications include *Ethics and Theology of Liberation* (1978); *History of the Church in Latin America 1492–1979* (1981); *Philosophy of Liberation* (1983).

VOLKER EID was born in 1940 in the Rhenish Palatinate and studied theology at Munich from 1960 to 1966. He was ordained to the priesthood in 1968 at Freising and was for many years active in pastoral work in Munich. From 1972 onwards he has been professor of moral theology at Bamberg University. His publications include: *Die Kunst in christlicher Daseinsverantwortung nach Theodor Haecker* (1968); (together with P. Hoffmann) *Jesus von Nazareth und eine christliche Moral. Sittliche Perspektiven der Verkündigung Jesu* (1975, third edition 1979). He is editor of the series *Moraltheologie— interdisziplinär* published by Grünewald-Verlag, Mainz.

KONRAD HILPERT was born in 1947. He teaches moral theology at the University of Duisburg. His publications include *Ethik und Rationalität. Untersuchungen zum Autonomieproblem und zu seiner Bedeutung für die theologische Ethik* (Düsseldorf 1980); articles in *Wörterbuch christlicher Ethik* ed. B. Stoeckle (Freiburg ^{2}1980), and in the fields of theology, catechetics, religious education, etc.

DIETMAR MIETH was born in Berlin in 1940. He is professor of theological ethics at the University of Tübingen. His chief publications are *Die Einheit von vita activa und vita contemplativa* (1969); *Dichtung, Glaube und Moral* (1976); *Epik und Ethik* (1976); *Moral und Erfahrung* (^{2}1979); (together with G. Stachel) *Ethisch handeln lernen* (1978); (ed.) *Meister Eckhart* (1979); *Gotteserfahrung—Weltverantwortung* (1982); *Zeitgemässe Unzeitgemässheiten, Grundzüge einer neuen Tugendlehre* (1982).

TONY MISFUD, SJ, was born in 1949 in Hamrun (Malta). He entered the Society of Jesus in 1965 and was ordained priest in 1979. He studied literature (Malta), philosophy (Italy) and theology (Chile and Spain), receiving his doctorate with distinction in moral theology at the Pontifical University of Comillas (Madrid) in 1980. Since 1974 he has worked in Chile where as well as pastoral work in working class parishes, he is professor of morals at the Catholic University of Chile (Santiago) and investigator of the CIDE (Centre for Investigation and Development of Education). He has contributed various articles to *Mensaje* (Chile), *Teologia y vida* (Chile), and *Moralia* (Madrid).

MARY CHRISTINE MORKOVSKY, CDP, was born in 1931. She is professor of philosophy at Our Lady of the Lake University, San Antonio, Texas. She has published numerous articles on metaphysics, moral philosophy, and Latin American philosophy of liberation.

ANTONIO MOSER was born in Brazil in 1939, studied theology in Lyons and at the Alphonsianum in Rome, where he took a doctorate in moral theology in 1972. He now lectures in moral theology in Petropolis and at the Catholic University of Rio de Janeiro. He has published books on responsible parenthood, the demographic problem and the ethical challenge of ecology, besides articles in various theological reviews.

BERNARD QUELQUEJEU, OP, is a Dominican. He edits *La Revue des Sciences philosophiques et théologiques* and lectures in anthropology and philosophical ethics at the Institut Catholique de Paris. His main works include *La Volonté dans la philosophie de Hegel* (1972), *Le Temps de la patience: Etude sur le témoignage* (1976) and *Le Manifeste de la liberté chrétienne* (1976). His numerous articles on moral philosophy and politics include a series on the subject 'Karl Marx a-t-il constitué une théorie du pouvoir d'Etat' in *La Revue des Sciences philosophiques et théologiques* 63 (1979).

FRANCISCO MORENO REJON, CSsR, was born in 1952 and is a Redemptorist priest. He studied theology and morals at Salamanca and Madrid universities, and since 1978 has been a parish priest in a working-class suburb of Lima. He has also been lecturing in moral theology at the Instituto Superior de Ciencias Morales in Lima since 1978. He has recently published studies on the ethic of liberation, in *Moralia*, and early man and ethics, in *Páginas*.

PHILIP ROSSI, SJ, was born in New York in 1943. He entered the Society of Jesus in 1962 and was ordained priest in 1971. He completed a Ph.D. in philosophy at the University of Texas at Austin in 1975. He has taught in the Theology Department at Marquette University, Milwaukee, Wisconsin (USA) since 1975 where he currently holds the rank of Associate Professor. His publications include *Together Toward Hope: A Journey to Moral Theology* (1983) and articles in *Journal of Religious Ethics, The Modern Schoolman, The New Scholasticism, Renascence,* and *The Thomist.*

LUISE SCHOTTROFF was born in 1934, in Berlin. She studied Protestant theology in Berlin, Bonn, Göttingen and Mainz, took her doctorate in Göttingen in 1960 and is now professor for new testament in Mainz. She is married and has one child. Her publications include: *Der Glaubende und die feindliche Welt. Beobachtungen zum gnostischen Dualismus und seiner Bedeutung für Paulus und das Johannesevangelium* (1970); (with W. Stegemann) *Jesus von Nazareth, Hoffnung der Armen* (1978); *Der Sieg des Lebens. Biblische Traditionen einer Friedenspraxis* (1982); and 'Die Schreckenscherrschaft der Sünde und die Befreiung durch Christus nach dem Römerbrief des Paulus' in *Evangelische Theologie* 39 (1979) 479–510.

DOMINIQUE STEIN was born in Paris in 1931. She qualified as a medical doctor in 1962, and she became registrar in the psychiatric hospitals of the district of the Seine, specialising in neuro-psychiatry. She became a psychoanalyst and a member of the Société psychanalytique de Paris between 1962–1975, and member of the Collège de Psychanalystes in 1980. She has published numerous articles on clinical practice and psychoanalytic theory (especially in *L'Inconscient* and *Etudes Freudiennes*) and has also written for *Concilium* before. Two of her books are due to appear: a collection of her poems, *La Terre a gagné*, and a study of psychoanalytic readings of the Bible (*Travail du text, travail par le texte*).

MARCIANO VIDAL, CSsR, who was born in San Pedro de Trones (León, Spain) in 1937, is a Redemptorist priest, and a doctor of moral theology. He is a professor in Comillas University (Madrid) and in the Instituto Superior de Ciencias Morales (Madrid) of which, at the present time, he is also principal.

Professor Vidal has written a number of books on ethical subjects, including: *Moral del amor y de la sexualidad* (1971); *Moral de Actitudes* (3 vols.) (1974–1981); *El discernimiento ético* (1980); *Moral del matrimonio* (1980); *La educación moral en la escuela* (1981); *La moral laica en la sociedad secular* (1983).

THE WORLD'S RELIGIOUS TRADITIONS

Current Perspectives in Religious Studies

Essays in honour of Wilfred Cantwell Smith
edited by Frank Whaling

Wilfred Cantwell Smith is one of the outstanding scholars of our time whose work has had a transforming effect in the fields of Religious Studies and Theology. This collection of essays honours Professor Smith and makes original contributions to religious studies today.

Five contributors take Professor Smith's concepts of faith and tradition as a starting point in their essays on particular religions (Christianity, Judaism, Hinduism, the Muslim and the Confucian traditions). These are followed by seven essays which examine current approaches to the study of religion.

Contributors: **Frank Whaling, J. L. Mehta, Tu Wei-Ming, Louis Jacobs, George Williams, Annemarie Schimmel, John Hick, George Rupp, Seyyed Hossein Nasr, Raimundo Pannikkar, John Carman, Geoffrey Parrinder, Ninian Smart.**

'*A fascinating volume in the vanguard of exploration of proper orientation in the study of religion and religions ... essential reading for all engaged in theology and religious studies.*' Professor Cyril G. Williams, University of Wales

'*Anyone interested in the relationship between faith and tradition in the world's major religions, in the future of inter-faith encounter, and in the rapprochement between Religious Studies and Theology, will benefit from this collection of essays.*' Professor Edward Hulmes, Department of Theology, University of Durham

'*Some of the articles are important and memorable in themselves, and the book as a whole may well prove a significant landmark in the field.*' W. Montgomery Watt, Emeritus Professor of Arabic and Islamic Studies, University of Edinburgh

320pp   cased   £11.95

T & T CLARK LTD, 36 GEORGE STREET, EDINBURGH EH2 2LQ, SCOTLAND

CONCILIUM 1983

NEW RELIGIOUS MOVEMENTS

LITURGY: A CREATIVE TRADITION

MARTYRDOM TODAY

CHURCH AND PEACE

INDIFFERENCE TO RELIGION

THEOLOGY AND COSMOLOGY

THE ECUMENICAL COUNCIL AND THE CHURCH CONSTITUTION

MARY IN THE CHURCHES

JOB AND THE SILENCE OF GOD

TWENTY YEARS OF CONCILIUM— RETROSPECT AND PROSPECT

All back issues are still in print: available from bookshops (price £3.50) or direct from the publisher (£3.85/US$7.45/Can$8.55 including postage and packing).

T. & T. CLARK LTD, 36 GEORGE STREET, EDINBURGH EH2 2LQ, SCOTLAND

CONCILIUM

All back issues are still in print: available from bookshops (price £3.50) or direct from the publisher (£3.85/US$7.45/Can$8.55 including postage and packing).

T. & T. CLARK LIMITED
36 George Street, Edinburgh EH2 2LQ, Scotland

GOD IS NEW EACH MOMENT

Edward Schillebeeckx

IN CONVERSATION WITH
HUUB OOSTERHUIS & PIET HOOGEVEEN

An encounter with Edward Schillebeeckx the human face behind the great theologian. In response to the questions of his colleagues, he provides a fascinating and comprehensive overview of his intellectual development and the implications of the major themes of his work. The discussions cover a wide range of topics including his ideas about Jesus, the ministry and sacraments, the Scriptures, the Church's future, the feminist movement and the liberation of the poor.

'The interviewers take him through every phase of his life and work and elicit from him replies of remarkable interest and honesty. This book affords us valuable insights into the mind and writings of a truly great theologian.'

Doctrine and Life

'. . . lets the reader much closer to the man: he is very open and generous about his life and work; spontaneous, candid and lively in his reactions to the questions. It also brings out in a very natural way just how simple and deeply rooted Fr. Schillebeeckx's faith remains.'

The Tablet

144 pages £3.95 paperback

T. & T. CLARK LTD, 36 GEORGE STREET, EDINBURGH EH2 2LQ, SCOTLAND